W9-DAM-781

Better Homes & Gardens.

celebrate the SEASON

2023

contents

gifts

114 Show a big dose of love with personalized gifts you make by hand. No crafting experience is needed—we'll guide your every step! Recipients will love treasures like ribbon-lined trays and pinecone ornaments. You'll even learn some super-clever gift-wrap ideas!

kids

136 Young ones will love joining in the festivity prep making seasonal treasures from unexpected supplies like swimming noodles, alphabet beads, holiday candies, and even fishing bobbers. The projects are so much fun to craft—you'll want to join right in!

in a twinkling

Explore quick, creative projects and recipes for impromptu get-togethers.

Better Homes & Gardens

celebrate the SEASON 2023

DOTDASH MEREDITH CONSUMER MARKETING
Director of Direct Marketing-Books: Daniel Fagan
Marketing Operations Manager: Max Daily
Marketing Manager: Kylie Dazzo
Content Manager: Julie Doll
Senior Marketing Coordinator: Elizabeth Moore
Senior Production Manager: Liza Ward

WATERBURY PUBLICATIONS, INC.
Editorial Director: Lisa Kingsley
Creative Director: Ken Carlson
Associate Design Director: Doug Samuelson
Contributing Editor: Sue Banker
Contributing Copy Editor: Russell Santana, E4 Editorial Services
Contributing Proofreader: Christopher Carley
Contributing Food Stylist: Jennifer Peterson

BETTER HOMES & GARDENS® MAGAZINE
Editor in Chief: Stephen Orr
Executive Editor: Oma Blaise Ford
Creative Director: Jennifer D. Madara

Copyright© 2023 by Meredith Operations Corporation.
Des Moines, Iowa.
First Edition. All rights reserved.
Printed in the United States of America.
ISSN: 10980733 ISBN: 978-0-696-30325-8

Cherishing the Old, Embracing the New

When I think about our family Christmases, I can't help but think about the traditions we hold dear. They never get old—they are wonderfully familiar, full of warmth, and truly magical.

We always look forward to our house-trimming ritual, cranking up holiday carols as the box-passing train readies to move the bins of decorations from the basement to the main floor. Before long the empty tree branches effortlessly become a breathtaking display and the house transforms into a wonderland.

On Christmas Day, we hop in the car to deliver food bags to those who may need an extra dose of holiday cheer. It is the most humbling and heartwarming time of the entire year.

When we gather for our own holiday meal, we bow our heads, hold hands, and squeeze tight. We're touchy-feely like that, with hugs when we first gather and again when we depart. If there are more in between, all the better!

And then there are the holiday menus. The "have to haves" that we anticipate for weeks leading to the big day.

And while we love those repeated moments from year to year, the unexpected surprises are just as welcomed. Maybe it's a new recipe that thoroughly knocks off our Christmas socks. Or perhaps it's fancy "love you more" wraps beneath the tree. Or, just maybe, it's finding new ways to spend time together—crafting handmade decorations to give or enjoy ourselves. These "aha" moments are often the root of joyous new traditions.

Creating special holiday moments is what *Better Homes & Gardens Celebrate the Season* is all about. From the season of giving thanks to ringing in the new year, every page offers inspiring ideas to lovingly share with family and friends.

Enjoy learning new crafting techniques to make holiday trims and meaningful gifts. Discover incredible kitchen-tested recipes that have gotten an enthusiastic thumbs-up. And let the kids join in the fun with projects designed specifically for them. So much awaits!

Here's hoping that the ideas in *Celebrate the Season* bring even more joy to the holidays. And, that just possibly, it will inspire new holiday traditions for you and your family and friends.

Wishing you all the merriment of the season,

fall

A BEAUTIFUL TIME OF YEAR
Celebrate the change of seasons
with incredible decorations that
share its splendidness.

Seasonal Sensations

Faux or real, pumpkins continue to lend autumnal flair long after the night of costumes and candy.

THAT'S A WRAP

Good-bye, pumpkin guts and carving sets. Hello, yarn and hot-glue gun. Wrapping pumpkins and gourds in vibrant yarn gives them a modern spin to last all autumn. For the large pumpkin, wrap the entire surface with a thick coat of yarn. Use contrasting yarn colors to make large cross-stitches randomly on the base yarn. For the small top pumpkin, wrap in different directions using different colors and weights of yarn. For the banded pumpkin, weave yarns in and out of burlap to make a textured design. Fray the edges of the band and pin in place around the pumpkin. Or simply wrap colored yarn stripes around the pumpkin, covering stems, too, if desired.

SOPHISTICATED COATS
This pumpkin collection offers creative approaches to create one-of-a-kind autumn centerpieces.

A. The Butterfly Effect
Start with a couple coats of metallic spray paint. When paint is dry, apply a large vinyl sticker of a butterfly or the insect of your choice.

B. Heavy Metal
Bring on the glitz. Draw on the designs using a pencil and go over the designs using a mini hot-glue gun; let cool. Finish with multiple coats of metallic spray paint.

C. Argyle Art
Referring to the photo, use a pencil to make the locations for tacks on the pumpkin ribs. Press tacks into place. Knot string around a tack on the bottom row, then continue looping a string around tacks to create a diamond pattern.

D. Lace Collar
Use a marker to mark two dots on the pumpkin ribs and one dot centered on each section. Connect the dots as shown below. Finish with thinner lines on each side of a straight line.

NATURALLY ARTISTIC

Plucked from the great outdoors, dried fall foliage comes alive in artistic designs. Cover pumpkins with blossoms—or loosely line up dried pieces in sections—for beauty that can be preserved for seasons to come on a faux pumpkin. Create an owl from layered leaves and add flowerhead eyes. Decoupage single leaves on smaller specimens. Even the tiniest gourds look fabulous with seeds or dried naturals glued around the stems.

Filled with Thanks

As you gather this Thanksgiving, welcome guests with open arms, open hearts, and clever crafts to make everyone feel right at home.

TABLETOP TOPIARIES

Take artificial gourds to new heights by crafting them into clever topiaries. For each base, paint a small terra-cotta flowerpot with autumnal colors; let dry. Cut floral foam to fit snugly into the container leaving ½ inch open at the top. Gently push the foam piece into the container and mark the center. For the bottom trunk piece, cut a 6-inch length from a stick or dowel that is approximately ⅜" in diameter. Push the trunk into the center of the foam piece as far as possible until secure. Stabilize with hot glue if needed. Use an awl to poke a hole in the bottom of an artificial gourd. Enlarge the hole as needed using a pencil. Secure the gourd to the trunk with hot glue. To add more gourds, pull out the stem on all but the top gourd and use 3-inch-long trunk pieces to connect layers. Tie ribbons to the trunk as desired. Cover the floral foam with popcorn kernels.

DECOUPAGED DECOR

Thanksgiving paper napkins add seasonal flair to a plain papier-mâché pumpkin. Cut enough 1½-inch squares from paper napkin to cover the pumpkin; separate napkin design layer from lining if they pull apart. For a central design, cut a larger motif from napkin. Working in small areas at a time, brush decoupage medium onto the pumpkin. Add the colored napkin pieces to the surface, arranging checkerboard style, doing your best on the irregular surface. Add the focal design piece if desired. Brush the covered pumpkin with a coat of decoupage medium; let dry. Tie a ribbon bow. Hot-glue the bow and a pinecone by the stem.

PLEASE COME IN

In lieu of a wreath, frame a small seasonal plaque for greater impact. Use hot glue to attach the plaque to the back of a glass-free picture frame. Decorate the frame with faux gourds, mini pumpkins, berries, and leaves. Ribbons and a wood cutout complete the presentation.

PRETTY PLACE CARDS

Elevate place cards using foam-filled gourds as risers. Use a cutting board to protect the work surface. Lay a gourd on the board and cut a ½-inch slit along the top as shown. Cut a ½×1½-inch piece from white cardstock. For backing, cut a 1¼×2½-inch piece from decorative cardstock. Use a glue stick to adhere the white strip to the backer. Write the guest's name on the place card. Slip the card into the slit on the gourd.

IN YOUR FAVOR

Rescued from recycling, a can makes a sturdy container to share some homemade snacks. Trim a paper napkin to wrap around the container. Brush the outside of the container with decoupage medium; cover with the napkin piece and let dry. Paint a coat of decoupage medium on the napkin; let dry. Insert an autumn cellophane bag into the can and fill with desired snack mix or candy. Tie closed with ribbons.

Leather Treasure

Thrifted belts and leather sheets in various shades become modern and functional home decor. So whichever home accessory style you choose, you can select your leather components accordingly. From timeworn shabby chic to sleek modern, choosing the right leather for DIY projects is well worth the hunt.

WRAP IT UP

A dowel, wood round, and belt come together to make a high-impact candlestick. Cut a 1-inch-diameter dowel to a desired length (these are 9–11 inches). Using a hole saw, cut a 3-inch-diameter circle from 1-inch-thick plywood. Sand the pieces, stain, and let dry. Center the dowel on the circle and screw together from the bottom. Trim the belt into 3-inch-long pieces. Add interest by including the belt's original holes as shown in Photo A. Apply wood glue to the back of each piece and secure to the dowel, spacing them equally apart. Wrap painter's tape around the leather pieces to hold them in place while the glue dries. Tap a 2-inch finish nail into the center top of the dowel. Cut off the head of the nail and gently push a candle onto it.

A

HANDLE IT

Give yourself a helping hand by attaching a strap to the side of a charcuterie board. Cut a 12-inch-long piece of leather from a belt. Mark a line 1 inch from one corner of the cutting board's shorter side. Repeat on the opposite corner. Apply a small amount of wood glue on each pencil line. Position one end of the belt on the glue. Choose heavy-duty upholstery tacks with long shanks (the stem of the tack) to securely attach a handle as shown in Photo A. Using pliers to hold a tack shank in place, center the tack at the end of the leather and hammer in place. Repeat on the opposite end, allowing the leather to arch to create a handle. Wipe away excess glue and let dry. Repeat on the other side of the board for a second handle.

GET A GRIP

A few add-ons elevate a standard wood box. For a weathered look, paint a box with white acrylic paint and, when dry, lightly sand the surface, edges, and corners. Cut a leather strap or belt to 24 inches long. With the lid on the box, align one end of the leather strap flush with the bottom edge of one side of the box. Using pliers, grip the shank of an upholstery tack and gently hammer it into the strap and lid. Arch the strap and position on the opposite side of the box. Secure with a tack. Lightly pencil lines on the strap along the crease where the box and lid meet. Remove the lid from box. Cut on the lines with scissors. Glue the cut pieces to the box, aligning them with the lid strap.

HIGH-END HARDWARE

A leather wrap gives drawer pulls a whole new look. Lay the drawer handle with arms side up on a piece of leather. Mark ½ inch around the handle and cut out the rectangular piece. Cut a second piece the same size. On one piece, mark and cut small openings for each arm to fit snugly through. On the other piece, measure and mark dots ¼ inch apart and ⅛ inch from the edge around the perimeter. Punch out the dots with a rotary punch. A rotary leather hole punch, shown in Photo A, adjusts to make a hole size that best fits the thread or twine. Stack the punched leather piece onto the other piece and use the holes as a guide to repeat the punching process. Spray adhesive on the backs of both pieces and fit around the handle, lining up the edges and smoothing them together. With waxed thread and a needle, sew a blanket stitch around the perimeter. Knot the ends, tucking knots between the pieces to finish.

ON TIME

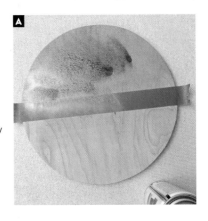

Transform a 12-inch wood round into a sleek clock. Drill a hole in the center of the wood round to fit the clock hands. Paint a white line slightly below the hole and let dry. Cover the white line with painter's tape and spray the top portion of the wood round gray. Get the texture of concrete using silver spray paint in a hammered finish as shown in Photo A. Let dry and remove tape. Set the wood round on a sheet of leather, trace a semicircle to fit the bottom portion, and cut out. Attach the leather piece to the wood round using spray adhesive. Measure and cut a strip of cowhide to fit around the edge of the wood clock. Glue and let dry. Install the clock motor and hands according to package instruction.

LACE UP

Simple stitching dresses up a plain vase. Wrap a sheet of leather around a cylinder vessel. Mark and cut to fit. Lay the leather sheet flat. Measure and mark dots ½ inch apart and ¼ inch from the edge up the side of the leather. Repeat on the opposite edge, making sure the dots align on each side. Use a rotary leather hole punch to make a hole on each mark. Lace the leather sheet together with waxed thread and parallel stitches. Once finished, tie off the end and slide the stitched leather tube of the vase.

BOHO BEAUTY

Dyed leather pieces string together to form an impactful wall hanging. Create your own triangle, circle, and semicircle patterns, or use found objects to trace and cut out shapes from a sheet of cowhide. Wearing rubber gloves, use a rag to massage leather dye into the front and back of each shape. Let dry. Punch a hole on the top and bottom of each shape with a rotary leather hole punch. Cut four 4-foot lengths of suede cord. Thread shapes onto three of the strands as shown in Photo A, leaving 6 inches of cord at the end to attach a tassel. Drill five holes equidistant apart through a branch or dowel. Tie and knot the three threaded strands through the three middle holes. Thread and knot the fourth cord through the end holes to become a hanger, leaving enough cord to attach tassels. Make five tassels from additional suede cord and tie onto ends. Space shapes as desired.

Captured in Clay

Enjoy everlasting likenesses of nature by sculpting, rolling, cutting, and shaping motifs from oven-dry clay.

BEAUTIFULLY BANDED

Create a textural focal point for a pillar candle that touts the beauty of the season. Cover the work surface with waxed paper. To craft the pinecone, hand knead metallic gold and brown oven-bake clay together just enough to get it to stick together. Twist the clay to achieve a marbled appearance. Shape the clay into a pinecone-shaped oval approximately ½ inch thick. Unfold a paperclip. Using the larger rounded end and starting at the bottom of the clay oval, press the paperclip into the clay and gently pull up to make a scale. Continue making scales, alternating placement, until the pinecone surface is all scales. Form a stem at the top and place onto a baking sheet; set aside. To make the greenery, roll green clay to a ⅛-inch thickness. Use a craft knife to cut a long diamond shape, approximately 3½ inches long. Remove from waxed paper and snip the edges, leaving ¼ inch in center uncut; place on baking sheet. Bake clay shapes in the oven according to manufacturer's directions. When cool, use instant glue to bond the pinecone to the greenery. Wrap a pillar candle with a piece of wide plaid ribbon; secure at seam with thumb tacks. Glue the pinecone motif to the front; let dry.

NATURE-KISSED

Dress a plain glass cookie jar for the fall season using just two colors of clay. Cover the work surface with waxed paper. From metallic gold air-dry clay, roll and shape three acorn shapes. From green clay, shape three acorn capes and gently press onto acorns. Use the non-serrated edge of a plastic knife to impress a cross-hatched pattern on each cap. Using an awl, make a ½-inch-deep hole in the top of each acorn. Roll three stem pieces, approximately ⅛-inch in diameter and 1 to 1½ inches long. Press the stem pieces into the acorn tops. Place on a baking dish. For leaf, roll green clay to ⅛-inch thickness. Use a crafts knife to cut out an oak leaf shape. Use the knife to impress veins in the leaf. Place onto the baking dish and bake according to manufacturer's directions. When cool, use instant glue to adhere the acorn motif to a glass cookie jar.

BERRY CUTE

Gift family and friends their favorite treats presented in beautiful containers that are super simple to make. Cover the work surface with waxed paper. Using two colors of purple air-dry clay, knead together until colors stick together. From clay, roll approximately a dozen ½-inch-diameter berries. Roll four berries from green clay. Place berries on a baking sheet. For leaves, roll out green clay to approximately ⅛ inch thick. Use a crafts knife to cut three leaf shapes, each approximately 2½ inches long. Use a plastic knife to impress leaf veins into each leaf. Place the leaves on the baking sheet and bake according to manufacturer's directions. When cool, use instant glue to adhere the berries and leaves to a small terra-cotta pot.

HOLD IT

Whether holding a special piece of jewelry on the dresser or wrapped candies on the dining table, this graphic leaf design is striking mounted on a pair of natural wood slices. Roll out two 3×4½-inch pieces of green oven-bake clay on a lined silicone mat or corrugated paper. Use a crafts knife to cut a D (half leaf) shape from each piece of clay. Gently join the leaf halves by pinching the straight edges together. Shape the ends into points. To enable the leaf to set upright, roll two small balls of clay for each side of the leaf and gently press onto the back of the leaf. Place the leaf on a baking dish and bake in the oven according to manufacturer's directions. Let cool. Use instant glue to attach the leaf to a pair of natural wood slices as shown.

Come One, Come All

If you find yourself far from home this Thanksgiving, spend the holiday with those nearby—friends, neighbors, coworkers—for a friendsgiving gathering that will make acquaintances feel like family.

MEALTIME MESSAGES

Instead of traditional place cards to mark where each guest will sit, assign a clutch of cookies to the task. Fasten a tuile to each gingerbread turkey with thin cotton string. A tuile is a thin, tube-shaped cookie, and it's the perfect holder for a message to each guest. Next, write those messages: On several slips of paper, jot down a reason you're thankful for each person, load the papers into the tuiles, and set one turkey-tuile combo on each plate. Let your guests circle the table and read the messages to decide which seat is meant for them.

PERSONALIZED PLACE SETTING

Strapped for time but want a handmade touch at each seat? Tie a knife, spoon, and fork in a bundle with red ribbon and raffia. Then use brown kraft paper as a place mat and give guests room to write things they are thankful for using marking pens.

MINI BANNER

Dress up a cheese pedestal or board with an easy-to-make banner. Fold a piece of paper in half and cut triangles at the fold. Write the word "cheese" on the folded paper triangles, arrange over twine, and staple in place. Tie the banner to wooden skewers and anchor in place using wood thread spools. Arrange fresh fruit that complements the cheese around the base of the pedestal or on the board for a tasty "cornucopia" centerpiece to each with the selection of cheeses.

Tabletop Ta-Das

PLATE CHARMER

Nothing says Thanksgiving like turkey Tom. To craft one for each place at the table, unfold a paper napkin once. Accordion-fold the napkin; secure at one end with a binder clip as shown. For the body, use a foam pear. To make eyes, use a pair of black map pins and push into place. For the beard, cut 2 inches off the end of a skinny red balloon. Cut a slit below the eyes and tuck the open end of the balloon into the slit. Cut wing shapes from napkin layers; pin on each side of pear. Use an O-ring to stabilize pear on plate. Place pleated napkin at the back of the pear, fanning out the tail feathers.

BUTTONED UP

Small paper treat cups get nudged into the special category with the addition of button accents. No need to find all the same buttons for each cup, using a variety lends interest to the Thanksgiving table.

DON'T LEAF 'EM GUESSING

Guide guests to their place at the table using festive fall leaves as markers. Carefully wash and dry leaves. Use acrylic paint to brush each guest's initial on a leaf; let dry. Tie a few faux berries to each stem using narrow coordinating ribbons.

SPECIAL TREATMENT

Keep the color palette rolling with custom napkin rings at each place setting. Use hot glue to attach ribbons to a plain napkin ring, layering as desired. Glue a group of stamens in fall colors to the ring, along with a small ribbon bow.

trims

MAKE HOME A PLACE
OF WARMTH AND JOY
Create lovingly made
decorations that share
the beauty of the season.

Just Hanging Around

Whether on the front door or gracing a wall, these easy-to-make arrangements make festive statements.

NATURE DROP

Mother Nature's originals inspired this beauty that can be pulled together in just minutes. Use an awl to make a small hole in the bottom center of several oversize pinecones. Twist a small screw eye into each hole. Tie narrow ribbon onto each screw eye. Arrange the pinecones and faux berried branches into a pleasing arrangement, keeping the ribbons taut. Use wire to secure the pinecones and branches together at the top of the arrangement. Cut off the excess ribbon and wire. Tie a multi-loop ribbon bow at the top; cut the tails shorter toward the center and leave them longer at the sides.

HOLIDAY HOLD UP

While a holiday tin would normally be found setting on a surface, it's an unexpected pleasure sighting one hanging on the wall. Before creating the arrangement, drill a pair of holes, side by side, on the top back side of the tin. Thread wire through the holes and make a loop for hanging. Place faux or real greens, berries, and snowy pinecones in the tin, adding a couple of traditional candy canes in the mix. Finish the wall piece with a pretty red velvet bow.

HONORING CHRISTMAS DAY

A grapevine wreath gets a grand makeover in the blink of an eye. In a well-protected work area, spray-paint the wreath white, allowing some of the branch color to show through; let dry. Spray-paint large wood or pressed cardboard numerals red; let dry. Brush the top surfaces of the numerals with decoupage medium and sprinkle artificial flake snow and let dry. On the lower right side, wire in snowy seasonal picks such as the pinecone and berry ones shown. For stability, use strong indoor/outdoor adhesive to bond the numerals together as shown. Glue the numerals centered at the wreath bottom.

VERY MERRY VINTAGE

Holiday boxes from an antiques store make a fun focal point for a gilded grapevine wreath. Decide on the box arrangement, adding a wrapped box for the foundation if needed. Hot-glue the boxes together as desired. Top small boxes with tiny bottlebrush trees for an added interest. Hot-glue the boxes to the wreath.

TRAY CHIC

A small metal serving tray hangs vertically from its handle to create a splendid backdrop for holiday greens. Wire together faux evergreen branches and pinecones to fill most of the tray. Use a hot-glue gun to adhere the grouping to the tray. Add a ribbon bow to the bottom stems and a couple of snowflakes, holding in place with hot glue.

Musically Inclined

As joyous as a Christmas carol, this music-themed decor hits all the right notes.

STAR PERFORMER

Musical instruments can bring joy even when totally silent. If you don't have a suitable instrument to use as a centerpiece, visit a secondhand shop or antiques store to find worthy options. This red accordion makes a grand statement surrounded by vintage holiday music books, jingle bells, bows, pinecones, and greenery. To make a sleighbell strap, cut off a segment from a leather belt. One with double prong holes allows the easy attachment of large silver glittered jingle bells every fourth hole using chenille stems. Thread narrow ribbons through the holes between the bells for colorful detail.

IN PERFECT HARMONY

From the trims on the tree to the holiday dinner table, let music inspire the decor. For the paper additions, if the real deal isn't at hand, check free images on the internet to reproduce sheet music and songbooks.

UPBEAT

Every dinner guest will feel incredibly special sitting down to a place setting manicured with such care. Start by using a spread of holiday sheet music as the place mat. Thread ribbon through a large jingle bell and place it on the napkin in the center of the plate. As the grand finale, tie a bow from music note ribbon. Wire a trio of jingle bells to the center. Rest the bow atop a few fresh greens at the top of the plate.

PARTING GIFTS

As you say your good-byes, send guests off with handcrafted favors. To make a bell ring, cut an 11-inch segment from a belt with a double prong hole design. Overlap the ends and aligning the holes, thread chenille stem through the holes, and twist ends to secure. Cut a 16-inch length of ¼-inch-wide ribbon. From the inside, thread ribbon ends through two adjacent holes next to bells; pull tails even. Cross ribbons to make an X and thread through the next set of holes. Continue making the cross-stitch pattern around the belt; knot ribbon tails on the inside and cut off excess. To make a treat cone, trace the pattern on page 154. Use the pattern to cut the shape from holiday music printed on cardstock. Shape the paper into a cone as shown; hot-glue the overlapping pieces to secure. From a 12-inch square of red glitter paper, cut a thin strip from one edge using pinking shears. Glue the trim around the paper edge and a holiday button below the spot where the sheet music overlaps in the center. Hot-glue silver chenille stem around the button. Tie a ribbon bow and hot-glue it below the button.

PRETTY AS A PICTURE

Vintage caroling images from songbooks, sheet music, greeting cards, or postcards make wonderful art for ornaments. Cut out the design and use a glue stick to attach it to red glitter paper; trim a narrow border. Layer the papers on white glitter paper; trim using pinking shears. Use a paper punch to make a hole at the top center. Add stickers to enhance the design. Thread ribbon through the hole; knot the ends together.

SHEET MUSIC ORNAMENT

Cut two 4×12-inch pieces of sheet music; accordion fold each piece every ½ inch. Place the two folded stacks side by side; tie the stacks together in the center. Use glue stick to adhere the stack ends together. Fan out the pleats. Place crafts glue on a paper plate; dip the outer edges into the glue. While wet, sprinkle the glue with silver glitter. Embellish the center with paper snowflakes, a metal-edge tag, stickers, and silver chenille stem. Punch a hole in the top of the snowflake. Thread the hole with cord; knot ends.

JINGLE BELL SWAG

An evergreen clipping gets holiday ready with the addition of a trio of jumbo jingle bells. Tie each bell to the end of 16-inch pieces of ribbon. Thread ribbon through large springs; knot ends together. Wire the ribbons to the greens. Tie a ribbon bow at the top.

Merry Melting

Feel like a kid again coloring on plastic drinking cups that melt in the oven to make darling discs to use in all sorts of ways. Experiment with different cup brands and oven temperatures, ranging from 250°F to 500°F. Some lightweight plastic cups melt into perfect circles while others tend to lose their shape. Doing an oven test before putting your artistic talents to work keeps renditions from going to waste.

DARLING DUO

On the bottom of a disposable clear plastic cup, use permanent marking pens to draw a snowman face as shown in Photo A. On the cup side, draw a scarf below the face as shown in Photo B. Draw stick arms to the sides, and a hat at the top as shown in Photo C. On a foil-lined pan, bake the cup (bottom up) at 500°F or as pretested. Do not leave unattended, and remove from oven as soon as cup melts flat as shown in Photo D. When cool, remove from foil. Use instant glue to adhere the disc to stiff white felt; trim a ¼-inch border with pinking shears. Hot-glue silver chenille stem around the plastic disc. Tie a ribbon bow to small faux holly; glue to the lower right side of the design. Use a small paper punch to make a hole through the felt at the top of the ornament. Thread with baker's string for hanging.

PACKAGE PRETTY

As soon as this gift is open, this lovely package topper is sure to get promoted to a special branch on the Christmas tree. To make the trim, draw a holiday design on the bottom and side of a disposable clear plastic cup using a permanent red marking pen. On a foil-lined pan, bake the cup (bottom up) at 500°F or as pretested. Do not leave unattended and remove from oven as soon as cup melts flat. When cool, remove from foil. Use instant glue to adhere the disk to stiff white felt; trim a 1½-inch border with pinking shears. Shape a red-and-white chenille stem to fit around the plastic disk; twist ends together and cut off excess leaving 1-inch-long tails. Hot-glue the chenille stem circle around the disk. Hot-glue silver chenille stem around the red-and-white one. Glue faux berries by the chenille stem tails as shown. Coil a 1-inch piece of silver chenille stem; hot-glue atop the berry wires. Use a small paper punch to make a hole through the felt at the top of the ornament. Thread with cord for hanging.

TOTALLY ORNAMENTAL

Create unique holiday cards that will leave recipients wondering how you made their timely treasure. To make a card, use permanent marking pens to draw a holiday design on the bottom and one-third up the side of a disposable clear plastic cup. On a foil-lined pan, bake the cup (bottom up) at 500°F or as pretested. Do not leave unattended and remove from oven as soon as cup melts flat. When cool, remove from foil. Centering the design, draw a 2½-inch-diameter circle. Use pinking shears to cut out the circle just within the drawn ring. Use instant glue to adhere the disk to stiff white cardstock; trim a ½-inch border with pinking shears. Glue the cutout to red cardstock; trim a ¼-inch border. Cut a 2½-inch length each of ⅜ and ⅝-inch-wide ribbon. Glue the narrow ribbon on the wider ribbon. Aligning one end with the top center edge of a 5×7-inch white cardstock card, glue in place. Adhere the ornament to the card, centering left to right and overlapping the ribbons ½ inch. Tie a contrasting ribbon bow; glue to top of ornament. Write the desired sentiment inside the card.

CAN DO

Super special packaging that looks like it took hours to create can be made in minutes and for just pennies. To make the focal point, draw holiday designs on the bottom and side of a disposable clear plastic cup using a permanent marking pens. On a foil-lined pan, bake the cup (bottom up) at 500°F or as pretested. Do not leave unattended and remove from oven as soon as cup melts flat. When cool, remove from foil. Place a tin can, such as a clean peanut can or quart paint can, on its side on the foil. Rest a metal spoon in the can to keep it from rolling. Arrange flattened disk on can. Place tray back in oven just until the disk melts to the shape of the can; remove from oven. Use instant glue to attach the colored design to the side of the can. Use hot glue to frame the design with cording.

Black and White and Gold All Over

Break away from traditional holiday hues to enjoy a refreshing palette that is totally unexpected.

IN STITCHES

For fun-to-make Christmas tree ornaments, turn to wool dryer balls to get things rolling. Dryer balls provide a soft surface for stitching ease. To mark the center where the band will go, place a rubber band around the ball. For the bottom half, thread an embroidery needle with gray embroidery floss and knot one end. Insert the needle by the rubber band and bring it back up anywhere below the rubber band. For stitching directions, refer to the illustrations on page 152. Make a French knot. Continue making French knots on the bottom half of the ball until the desired look

is achieved. Bring the floss back up near the rubber band, knot floss, and cut off excess. For the top half, thread the needle with cream embroidery floss and knot one end. Insert the needle just above the rubber band and bring back up nearby. Make running-stitch vines around the top. Add lazy daisy leaves and petals to the vines. Remove the rubber band. Cut a ⅝×11-inch piece of fabric. Attach it to the ball, where the rubber band was, using gold embroidery floss and cross-stitches. To hang the ornament, sew an embroidery floss loop at the top.

PRETTY PERCH

A wreath of fluffy yarn pom-poms is the perfect landing place for a sweet lifelike bird. To make a pom-pom, use lids and other round items to trace circles onto cardboard. Trace a larger circle with a smaller circle inside to make a donut shape. The larger circle determines the diameter of the finished pom-pom. This wreath used three sizes of pom-poms. Cut out the larger circles. Cut a ⅛-inch slit to the center circle; cut out the center. Wrap yarn around the ring. Hold the end of the yarn in place while wrapping to secure it. Wind yarn around the entire ring until full and the center circle is nearly filled in. Cut off the yarn tail, then start snipping through the wrapped yarn all along the edge of the ring. Be sure to cut through every strand of yarn. Cut a 12-inch piece of yarn and tie it around the middle of the

pom-pom, close to the ring. Tie the yarn once, then wrap the ends around to the other side, pull tight, and knot. Remove the cardboard ring. Trim the cut yarn tails and pom-pom ends, if needed, to shape. Cut a 13½-inch circle from white posterboard. Cut an 8-inch circle from the center. Hot-glue pom-poms to the circle until covered and the wreath looks uniform. Cut a 5×24-inch piece of flannel, trimming the ends into rounded points; set aside. Spray one side of a 14-inch diameter wood circle with adhesive and press onto a piece of plaid fabric; let dry. Trim off the excess fabric. Use hot glue to attach the pom-pom wreath to the plaid fabric circle, keeping the plaid straight with the bow at the top. Hot-glue a couple of silvery picks to the opening of the wreath. Decide the placement for the bird and hot-glue it to the picks.

SEW SPECIAL

Make Christmas morning even more magical with handmade stockings holding Santa's gifts.

WHAT YOU NEED
Tracing paper
Pencil
Scissors
⅓ yard of plaid flannel shirting fabric
¼ yard of gold flannel shirting fabric
⅓ yard of medium-weight fusible interfacing
Iron
Sewing pins
Fabric scissors
Sewing machine
Matching sewing thread
Sewing needle
Buttons in 1¼ and 1 inch diameters

WHAT YOU DO

1. Trace the stocking and cuff patterns on page 153. Use the stocking pattern to cut 2 shapes from plaid fabric and 2 from fusible interfacing. Fold cuff fabric in half as per the pattern; cut one cuff piece.

2. Lay plaid stocking pieces on an ironing surface, wrong sides up. Place a fusible interfacing piece atop each one; adhere following manufacturer's directions.

3. Pin stocking front to back, right sides facing. Using ½-inch seam allowance, stitch around the sides and bottom of the stocking leaving the top open.

4. Using fabric scissors, snip along the edges approximately every 2 inches, being cautious not to cut through seams. Turn right side out. Fold over a ½-inch cuff; press.

5. For binding, cut a 1¼×40-inch piece of fabric. Press under ¼ inch on each long edge. Align folded edges; press. Pin binding around stocking and use a zigzag stitch to secure. Remove pins.

6. To make the cuff, fold the cuff fabric (right sides facing) as shown on the pattern. Using a ½-inch seam allowance, sew around the cut edges, leaving a 3-inch opening at one end. Trim the seam and clip the curves. Turn the cuff right side out; press. Hand-stitch the opening closed.

7. Wrap the cuff around the stocking, overlapping on the front as shown; pin in place.

8. To back the buttons, cut a 1½×10-inch piece of fabric. Machine-baste along one long edge. Gather the fabric and shape into a circle; knot thread ends together and stitch seam together.

9. Place the fabric ring on the cuff, top with layered buttons, and sew through the cuff to secure.

10. Hand-stitch the stocking to the cuff on the inside of the stocking. Remove the pins.

11. To make the hanger, cut a 5×1¼-inch piece of fabric. Press under ¼ inch on each long edge. Align folded edges; pin together. Stitch along open edge to secure. Overlap ends and hand-stitch to the inside of the cuff.

DRESSED TO IMPRESS

Embrace this regal palette and decorating style by carrying it through to holiday gift wrapping. Choose a variety of black and white papers for a cohesive look and let creativity shine by making each package embellishment uniquely amazing. Use these classy examples to inspire your own finishing touches.

WINTRY WRAP

Spiff up a plain glass candleholder or jar in a jiffy by adding a festive fabric tie. Cut a wide band long enough to wrap the vessel plus 8 inches for the tails. Trim the tails to a rounded point and tie onto the vessel. Use the container to hold candy canes in the color scheme or place a candle inside.

BELLS 'N' BERRIES

An alternative to a napkin ring, this cord tie is perfect for any winter dinner. To make a tie, cut a 20-inch length of gray cord. Cut two 1-inch pieces of wire; fold each in half. Thread a jingle bell on each wire and slide to the fold. Hold the wires of one jingle bell next to a cord end, wrap with tape to hold in place and to keep the cord from fraying. Repeat on the other end of the cord. Conceal the tape by wrapping ivory embroidery thread around it. When done, knot the floss around the cord and cut off excess. To place around napkin, fold the tie in half. Lay the napkin on the tie. Thread the jingle bell ends through the loop in the cord and cinch as desired. Tuck faux berries into the tie for a colorful accent.

TASSEL TIE

Pair a silky tassel (see illustration on page 152), handcrafted in your nontraditional color scheme, with silver seasonal charms to tie on party stemware. Guests will easily keep track of their glasses using the unique charms as identifiers.

AWAITING SANTA

Created to conceal bottles, round elongated gift containers make fun stand-ins for holiday stockings. Jazz up the handle with the addition of a multi-loop bow and a sprig of artificial berries. For personalization, tie on a glittered pressed board initial.

Totally Unexpected

With a little imagination, decorative boxes can be used for so much more than instant gift containers.

AT YOUR SERVICE

Holiday boxes do double duty as cheerful snack serving containers. Before using, line the box with tissue paper and add a second layer of parchment paper, using holiday-themed punches to add cutouts around the edges.

LOSE THE LID

Instead of seeing the stems in a floral arrangement, offer something much more festive. To use a bottle box as a vase, remove the lid. Trim the box with ribbons, chenille stems, and a bow. Place a plastic or glass vessel in the box for stability. Arrange flowers and greenery in the vase. If using fresh items, carefully add water to the vessel.

LEG LIFT

Create a jolly side table from a holiday hat box that not only looks cute, but also offers extra storage. To make one, purchase a wood round that is slightly smaller than the box. Measure and mark four equidistant leg positions on the wood, approximately 1 inch from the edge. Attach the legs to the wood round following the leg manufacturer's directions. Turn over the box. Use wood glue to attach the wood round to the center of the box; let dry.

Ten-Minute Vintage Trims

Gather the family together and whip up a tree-full of darling ornaments in just one evening.

MEMORY BOOK

Children's holiday book covers from years past are full of personality. Make miniature versions by opening the book and photocopying the front and back covers at 50% onto cardstock. Trim around the edge. Cut pages from four sheets of printer paper, slightly smaller than the front/back cover piece. With the cover side down, neatly stack the pages centered on top. Hold the stack firmly and use a long-neck stapler to secure pages together in the center of the spine and near each end. Fold the book in half. Make a hanging loop from a 4-inch length of cord. Hot-glue the ends in the center of the book near the top edge. Tie a ribbon bow to the cord.

FROM THE JEWELRY BOX

Connect two pine chenille stems by twisting together at one end. Wind the chenille stem to make a 3-inch-diameter wreath. Fold the ends under to secure in place. Clip a vintage earring on each side. Complete the mini wreath ornament with a velvet ribbon hanger.

COOL SPOOL

A large thread spool, originally stained green, offers a stage for a tiny wintry scene. Tie a ribbon bow around the spool. For the top display, use small vintage trims, such as bottlebrush trees, plastic animals, or toys. Hot-glue the arrangement to the spool. No hanger needed, simply set the trim on the branches of the holiday tree.

JOLLY CANDY CUP

Glass or plastic, antique Santa mugs bring playful charm to the tree. Cut a 16-inch length of holiday cord for the hanger; knot each end to prevent raveling. Thread one end through the cup handle; knot ends together leaving 1½-inch tails. Use extra-strong instant adhesive to glue the loop end inside the cup, opposite the handle. Let the glue dry, then reinforce the bond with strong tape. Fill the cup with wrapped holiday candy.

Enhancing Nature

With a little bit of paint and creativity, nature's treasures lay the foundation for one-of-a-kind holiday crafts.

'SNO GUY LIKE GORDY

A dried gourd offers a unique shape for a wintry friend. Choose yarn in all your favorite colors to put a personal spin on his striped stocking hat.

WHAT YOU NEED
Kraft paper
Spray primer
Clean dried gourd in desired shape
Deep turquoise spray paint
Acrylic paints in white, orange, and black
Cardboard scraps
Terry dishwashing pad
Hot-glue gun and glue sticks
Yarn in desired colors, sizes, and textures
1-inch-diameter adhesive chair glides
⅜-inch-diameter adhesive rubber bumpers
Jar lid, optional

WHAT YOU DO
1. In a well-ventilated work area, cover the surface. Spray primer on the dried gourd; let dry. Spray on a coat of turquoise paint as shown in Photo A. Let the paint dry.

2. Place some white paint on a piece of cardboard. Dip a terry dishwashing pad into the paint and very lightly dab the paint onto the gourd, allowing some of the blue to show through as shown in Photo B. Continue painting in this manner until the bottom half of the gourd is covered; let dry.

3. To create the hat, hot-glue the yarn end on the back side of the gourd where the bottom of the hat will start. Run a line of hot glue around the gourd and attach the first two rounds for the hat as shown in Photo C. Continue winding yarn up the gourd, changing colors as desired, tacking with hot glue to hold in place. Wind several layers at the end to create the look of a pom-pom.

4. Press chair glides on the gourd front, positioning as eyes and a nose. Use rubber bumpers to create a smile as shown in Photo D.

5. Paint the nose orange. Paint the eyes and smile pieces black as shown in Photo E. Let the paint dry.

6. Paint snowy eyebrows over the eyes as shown in Photo F. To give features a snowy appearance, paint the tops white. For highlights, dip the paintbrush handle into paint and dot onto the eyes and mouth as shown in Photo G. Let the paint dry.

7. If the gourd tends to tip, steady it in a jar cap.

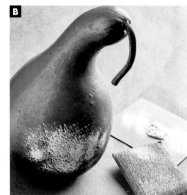

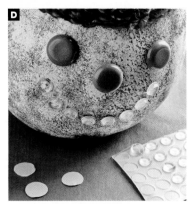

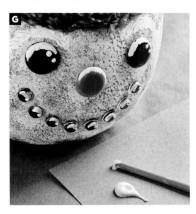

RISE TO THE OCCASION

No one would guess that underneath this pretty patina lies half of an earthy, all-natural, hard-as-wood gourd. To make the pedestal dish, start with a clean, dry gourd. Saw off a bowl-shaped section. Clean out the insides and sand the edges. For the base, use instant glue to adhere an empty adhesive tape spool (or thread spool) to the center of a 4-inch-diameter wood disc (see supplies in Photo A). Glue the base to the gourd. Spray the inside of the gourd with primer; let dry. Spray-paint the inside of the gourd white. When dry, turn the gourd upside down. Paint the outside of the dish in the same manner as for the snowman, steps 1 and 2, on page 65. Let the paint dry. Line the dish with white garland and nest pretty holiday bulbs inside.

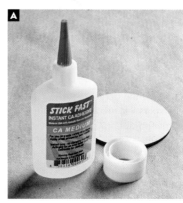

PAINTED PINECONE WREATH

Make a pretty pinecone wreath for the holidays (or any time of year!) with an inexpensive grapevine wreath, spray paint, and a few other basic craft supplies. When using real pinecones, dust off any debris. Lay down a drop cloth to protect the work surface. In a well-ventilated area, spray a coat of primer on the pinecones. Let them dry. Spray the primed pinecones the desired colors. To achieve an ombre effect, use paints within a few shades of each other. The wreath in the photo used a mix of blues with small pops of silver. Let the pinecones dry. Use hot glue to attach the pinecones to a wire wreath form, starting with the darkest pinecones and working up to the lightest pinecones.

Note: To make a wreath last longer, use floral wire to attach the pinecones after positioning them with glue. This prevents the pinecones from falling off in extreme weather conditions.

Cozy & Cute

A touch of farmhouse nostalgia in these decorations expresses the sensibility of traditional family gatherings. Natural and vintage materials warm the scene.

HOME, SWEET HOME

With the charm and detail of a gingerbread house, this sweet structure relies on felt, lacy trims, beads, and embroidery floss to cook up a sentimental favorite. Outfit it with a bead-embellished Christmas tree or personalize the accents. Buttons, pom-poms, and other white trims can capture the look of a snowy cottage.

WHAT YOU NEED

Felt in tan and white
2¾-inch scrap of ¼-inch-wide white rickrack trim
Hot-glue gun and glue sticks
Sewing thread in tan and white
Sewing needle
Embroidery needle
⅛-inch beads in white and brown
Embroidery floss in tan and white
¾-inch-diameter snowflake button, optional
Small white pom-poms, optional
2-inch scrap of white trim, optional
Polyester fiberfill
Tan cord, optional

WHAT YOU DO

1. Trace the patterns, page 154, onto white paper; cut out. For one house, trace two front/back walls, two side walls, and one floor onto tan felt. Trace a roof, desired tree shapes, and a window (optional) onto white felt. Trace door onto white or tan felt. Cut out shapes.

2. For tan door, hot-glue rickrack trim around outside edge; hot-glue door to house front. Using white sewing thread, stitch a white bead to door for a doorknob. Refer to page 152 for stitch diagrams, For white door, blanket-stitch door to house front using two strands of tan embroidery floss; leave bottom edge unstitched. Using tan thread, stitch a brown bead to door for doorknob.

3. Hot-glue desired tree to house front. Stitch brown beads to one-piece tree using white thread. Referring to photo, use one strand of tan floss to stitch running stitches on three-piece tree. Using two strands of white floss, stitch a star stitch at top of tree.

4. Using white sewing thread, blanket-stitch the floor to bottom edges of house front and back.

5. Hot-glue a snowflake button or window, pom-poms, and/or white trim to house front. Straight-stitch windowpane dividers using two strands of tan floss. Blanket-stitch around window with tan floss.

6. Blanket-stitch bottom edge of each side wall to floor using white sewing thread. Blanket-stitch side edges of house front and back to side walls with white thread.

7. Stuff house with polyester fiberfill. Run a line of hot glue along the roofline of house and attach roof to house leaving ¼-inch of roof overhanging front wall.

8. If desired, stitch cord through roof peak. Knot ends to make a hanging loop.

RING THE BELLS

Tucked Into an evergreen wreath, these homespun bells ring out a seasonal welcome. Made of grain sack fabric, the bells possess a textural attraction that belies their neutral color. With jingle bells and a striped bow as finishing touches. The bells stand out on a front door or in any nook that needs a little holiday flair. To make the bells, enlarge the pattern on page 155 on white paper; cut out. Trace the pattern onto gray grain sack fabric for the fronts. Trace the pattern onto linen for the backs. Cut out the bell shapes. Sew together pieces with right sides facing, leaving a 4-inch opening along the bottom of the bell. Stuff each bell with polyester fiberfill. Hand-sew the opening closed. Hand-stitch jingle bell to bottom center of fabric bell. Stitch a length of twine through the top of the bell. Knot the ends to make a hanging loop.

WOODLAND COUNTDOWN

Surprise the family with an adventure each day of December. Tuck activity tags behind snowflake-embellished wood slices and flip over a slice to reveal a plan for the day. Fun and games can mingle with volunteer opportunities. The Advent calendar's tree-decorated slice marks the arrival of Christmas.

WHAT YOU NEED

12-inch square wooden plank plaque
0.8-inch right-angle screw hooks
1-inch wooden numbers 1 through 25
24 wooden snowflakes
1 wooden tree
White acrylic paint
Foam paintbrush
Crafts glue
Twenty-five 2-inch-diameter predrilled
     wood slices
Twenty-five 1½-inch-diameter round
     kraft tags
4×6-inch burlap bag
Hot-glue gun and glue sticks

WHAT YOU DO

1. Mark the placement of the holes for the hooks on the plank plaque. Make the top row of five marks ½ inch below the top edge, 1¼ inches from each side edge, and 2⅜ inches apart. Mark hook placements in rows two, three, and four, 2¼ inches below the marks in the row above. Mark hook placements in row five 2⅜ inches below the placement marks in row four. Screw a hook into the plaque at each mark.

2. Paint the wooden numbers, snowflakes, and tree white; let dry. Use crafts glue to adhere a number to one side of each wood slice. Use crafts glue to adhere a number to one side of each wood slice. Glue a snowflake to the opposite side of each wood slice numbered 1 through 24. Glue the tree to the opposite side of the wood slice numbered 25. Hang embellished slices in order on hooks.

3. Handwrite an activity on 24 of the round kraft tags. Hang activity tags behind wood slices 1 through 24. Write Advent Activity Tags on a round kraft tag and use hot glue to adhere it to the burlap bag. Store activity tags inside the bag.

LINEN AND LACE

With the aura of yesteryear, these linen stockings await Santa's visit. Lacy doilies decorate the heels to personalize each stocking. Layer on one or more vintage or new doilies to dress up each stocking. A dip in a tea bath and a quick rinse can add age to doilies that appear a little too white or new looking. Scour flea markets and thrift stores for bargain doilies. A stain on one edge isn't a problem. Clip it off and use the undamaged section.

WHAT YOU NEED
Fabric scissors
⅓ yard of linen in desired color
⅓ yard of medium-weight fusible interfacing or fusible fleece
⅓ yard of muslin
Crocheted doilies
Straight pins
Cream sewing thread
Sewing needle

WHAT YOU DO
1. Enlarge the patterns, page 155, onto white paper.
2. From linen, cut 1 each of stocking pattern and stocking pattern reversed, and a 1¼×5-inch strip.
3. From fusible interfacing or fusible fleece, cut 1 each of interfacing pattern and interfacing pattern reversed.
4. From muslin, cut 1 each of stocking pattern and stocking pattern reversed.

5. Following manufacturer's instructions, press an interfacing stocking onto the wrong side of a corresponding linen stocking front and back, leaving a ½-inch fabric border around the edges of the interfacing.
6. Place a doily on right side of stocking front over the heel area; pin. Trim excess doily flush with raw stocking edges. Using cream sewing thread, hand-stitch doily in place.
7. For hanging loop, fold the 1¼×5-inch linen strip in half lengthwise with wrong sides together; press. Open the strip and fold long edges into center crease; press. Fold strip in half, enclosing long raw edges inside strip; press. Topstitch strip closed.
8. To assemble stocking, sew together stocking front and back, leaving top edge open. Carefully trim half of seam allowance around the sides and bottom of stocking to reduce bulk. Clip curves by snipping seam allowance close to the stitch line every ½ inch. Turn stocking right side out; press.
9. For lining, sew together muslin stocking and stocking reversed, leaving top edge open and a 4-inch opening for turning along bottom edge. Do not turn lining right side out. Trim seams and clip curves of lining.
10. Fold the hanging loop crosswise in half and pin ends to top edge of heel side of stocking body, aligning raw edges.
11. Insert stocking body into lining stocking. Sew together on top raw edges. Turn all layers right side out through opening in lining; hand-sew opening in lining closed. Insert lining into stocking and press flat.
12. Using a ⅛-inch seam allowance, topstitch around top opening of stocking.

Happy Go Lucky

The joy of a snowy day shines from this jolly trio.

FAMILY OUTING

Dressed in coordinating painted, faux fur, and fabric apparel, each family member flaunts individual personality. A sturdy foil-based foundation grounds the clay-wrapped figures. Replicate this group or make a snow figure to represent each member of your family. Roll plenty of snowballs to finish the scene.

WHAT YOU NEED

18-inch roll of aluminum foil
Crafts glue
Toothpicks
Air-dry clay
Fine-grit sandpaper
Acrylic paint in off-white, black, orange, pink, red, and dusty blue
Artists' brushes
Clear acrylic matte spray finish
Decoupage medium
Clear fine glitter
Scraps of knit fabric in red, multicolor strip, and black
Scraps of faux fur in brown and white
Fabric glue
Red knit fabric glove
½-inch buttons: 4 red and 3 red-and-white polka-dot
¾ yard of ¼-inch red trim
Water-soluble marking pen
Small knit flower
½ yard of ½-inch red ribbon
Miniature metal pail
½ yard of ⅛-inch red trim
Two ⅛-inch red buttons

WHAT YOU DO

1. To make the armatures, tear off several 12×18-inch pieces of foil for ear armature. Tear off more pieces as needed.

2. Snowman and snow woman armatures: Fold a piece of foil in half lengthwise for each armature. Roll and compress each piece into an egg shape. Add firmly packed foil layers until each body is 8½ inches tall. For each head, tightly roll a piece of foil into a ball. Add more foil until each head is 1½ inches across.

3. Snow child armature: Make body and head in same manner as for snowman and snow woman until body is 5 inches tall and head is 1¼ inches across.

4. Add crafts glue to the top of a body and to one end of a toothpick. Push glued end of toothpick into body. Add crafts glue to remaining end of toothpick and push corresponding head onto toothpick as shown in Photo A. Firmly press together head and body as shown in Photo B. Repeat with remaining body and head pieces.

5. For each snowman and snow woman arm, roll and press foil pieces into a 3-inch-long log that is ¾ inch in diameter. For each snow child arm, roll and press foil pieces into a 2-inch-long log that

is ½ inch in diameter. Shape and bend each arm at elbow, as desired. Shape and bend snow child body and head as desired. For each snowman and snow woman leg, roll and press foil pieces into a 2-inch-long log that is 1 inch in diameter. For each snow child leg, roll and press foil pieces into a 1¼-inch-long log that is ¾ inch in diameter. Join each arm and leg to corresponding body using crafts glue and half of a toothpick as shown in Photo A.

6. To cover the armatures with clay, follow manufacturer's instructions; prepare a small handful of air-dry clay. Apply a thin layer of clay to legs and upper body as shown in Photo C, dipping your fingers in water and smoothing clay.

7. Make sure clay fits tightly against the foil. Work clay up the body, covering the armature. Smooth any gaps or seams with moistened fingertips. Let dry completely. Repeat for each armature.

8. For each figure, roll a carrot-shaped clay nose and two small balls of clay for cheeks; place on the face, blending edges with moistened fingertips until smooth. Add more clay to figure to fill any small cracks, if needed. Let dry overnight.

9. Roll small pieces of air-dry clay into various sizes of snowballs; let dry.

10. Lightly sand each figure and the snowballs; wipe off sanding dust. Paint the figures and snowballs off-white; let dry. Lightly sand figures and snowballs; apply second coat of off-white. Dip brush handle tip into black paint to make dots for eyes; let dry. Dip a toothpick into off-white and dot each eye with a highlight. Dip a small brush handle tip into black paint to make dots for each mouth. Paint noses orange. Dry-brush cheeks using pink.

11. Apply several coats of clear acrylic spray finish to each figure, allowing finish to dry after each coat.

12. Brush decoupage medium over snowballs; roll in clear glitter.

13. To dress the snowman, cut a 5×7-inch strip from red knit fabric for hat. With right sides together, hand-sew short ends

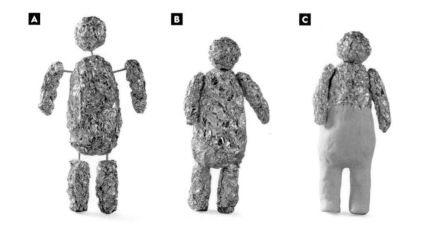

A B C

together to make a tube. Make a running stitch along one edge; pull ends to gather the top and tie off. Cut a small circle of brown faux fur and use a running stitch to gather the edge; pull thread tightly and tie off, making a small pom-pom. Using fabric glue, adhere pom-pom to top of hat. Roll up brim. Place crafts glue inside hat and attach to snowman's head.

14. Cut two fingertips from red glove, each about ½ inch long. Glue fingertips to ends of snowman arms for mittens.

15. Use a pencil to make four dots down front of snowman. Add crafts glue to backs of ½-inch red buttons and press one firmly to each dot.

16. Using fabric glue, adhere short strips of white faux fur around wrists for cuffs. Cut a 1¼×15-inch strip from multicolor stripe knit fabric for scarf. Tie and glue scarf around snowman's neck.

17. To dress the snow woman, refer to photo above. Paint the coat red. Paint mittens black. Let dry. Spray with clear acrylic spray finish; let dry.

18. Using fabric glue, adhere pieces of ¼-inch red trim around edges of coat and cuffs.

19. Trace patterns, page 156, onto white paper and cut out. Using a water-soluble marking pen, trace collar onto white faux fur; trace one hat crown and two hat brims onto black knit fabric. Cut out pieces. Use fabric glue to adhere collar around top of coat.

20. With right sides together and using a ¼-inch seam allowance, hand-sew the brim pieces together along the outside edge. Turn brim right side out. Make a running stitch around the edge of the hat crown, pull the tails to gather slightly. With right sides together, hand-sew the hat crown to the hat brim. Turn hat right side out. Place fabric glue inside hat and attach to snow woman's head. Glue knit flower to side of hat.

21. Glue three red-and-white polka-dot buttons to coat front. Tie red ribbon into a bow. Glue bow to top of coat front.

22. Paint metal pail red; let dry. Using a brush handle tip, add off-white polka dots

to paint; let dry. Using crafts glue, adhere snowballs inside pail. Glue pail to snow woman's hand.

23. To dress the snow child, refer to the photo above. Paint the coat dusty blue. Paint mittens red. Let dry. Spray snow child with clear acrylic finish; let dry.

24. Using fabric glue, adhere pieces of ⅛-inch red trim around edges of coat. Glue two ⅛-inch red buttons to coat front. Adhere short strips of white faux fur around wrists for cuffs. Cut a ⅞×8-inch strip from red knit fabric for scarf. Tie and glue scarf around snow child's neck.

25. Cut a 3×6-inch strip from red knit fabric for hat. With right sides together, hand-sew short ends together to make a tube. Make a running stitch along one edge; pull ends to gather the top and tie off. Cut a small circle of brown faux fur and use a running stitch to gather the edge; pull thread tightly and tie off, making a small pom-pom. Using fabric glue, adhere pom-pom to top of hat. Roll up brim. Place crafts glue inside hat and attach to snow child's head.

ONE CHILL FOX

Bundled up from ears to toes, this cool fox prowls the snowy landscape. Easy patterns and embroidery turn felt into a fashion-forward forest friend. The jute hanger complements the woodsy feel. Change the coat color and buttons to customize the ornament using your favorite hue.

WHAT YOU NEED

Felt in black, blue, peach, and white
Disappearing-ink marking pen
Embroidery floss in white, peach, black, and blue
Two black seed beads
Small artist's brush
Pink dye stick
Three light tan mini buttons
Jute
Crafts or fabric glue

WHAT YOU DO

1. Trace the patterns from page 156 onto white paper; cut out. Using a disappearing-ink marking pen, trace each shape onto appropriate felt color the number of times indicated on the patterns; cut out. Cut the body pieces from black felt.

2. Refer to the stitching diagrams on page 152 for help if needed. Use two strands of embroidery floss for all embroidery unless otherwise indicated.

3. Using white floss and referring to photo, straight-stitch the jagged edge of the tail tip to one tail piece. Blanket-stitch the tail pieces together using peach floss.

4. Place the face on a body piece then place the coat on top. Adjust face to fit inside face opening of coat; remove coat. Using peach floss, straight-stitch outer edge of face to the body piece.

5. Place the ears on the body piece, positioning short straight edge of each ear toward other ear. Using peach floss, blanket-stitch the ears to the body.

6. Using the coat for placement, place the cheeks on the face; remove coat. Using white floss, use tiny straight stitches to join cheeks to face.

7. Using one strand of black floss, stitch a bead to each cheek for an eye. Using black floss, straight-stitch a triangle between the cheek bottoms for a nose. Using a small brush, lightly brush pink dye onto cheeks.

8. Using blue floss and referring to photo, stitch large blanket stitches around the legs and feet, bringing stitches into center between legs and feet. Straight-stitch a vertical line through the center of the legs and feet.

9. Using black floss, straight-stitch the short edge of tail to back of coat near bottom. Pin coat to body. Using blue floss, blanket-stitch around coat edges and face opening.

10. Stitch buttons to center of coat front using black loss. Fold a 6-inch length of jute in half; glue ends to inside top edge of fox. Let dry.

11. Pin remaining body piece to back of fox ornament. Whipstitch together using black floss, making sure to conceal stitches in the layers to prevent show-through to front.

LLAMA LOVE

Hearts will beat faster at the sight of this blushing creature. Felt and embroidery floss combine for an easy-to-love ornament. Bedecked with a colorful harness, the llama shows off its heart on its saddle. Loop the harness with tassels or pom-poms in vivid colors to bring South American flair to a tree.

WHAT YOU NEED
Felt in ivory, teal, light teal, and red
Disappearing-ink marking pen
Embroidery floss in black, green, teal, red, and white
Embroidery needle
Beading needle
Seed bead in silver or red
6-inch length of bakers twine in red-and-white
Polyester fiberfill
Cosmetic blush

WHAT YOU DO
1. Trace pattern from page 157 onto white paper; cut out. Using a disappearing ink marking pen, trace each shape onto appropriate felt color the number of times indicated on the pattern; cut out.
2. Refer to page 152 for stitch diagrams. Use one strand of embroidery floss for all embroidery unless otherwise indicated.

3. Using black floss, stitch the eye with a few curving backstitches and the eyelashes with two straight stitches.
4. Align top of saddle with llama's back on one body piece. Using two strands of green floss, backstitch just inside the curved edge. Using matching floss, whipstitch heart to saddle. Using a beading needle and desired floss, stitch a seed bead to center of heart.
5. Pin together body pieces with wrong sides together. Place loose ends of baker's twine between layers for a hanging loop. Using white floss and catching twine ends in the stitching, whipstitch around the body; stuff llama with polyester fiberfill as you stitch, leaving an opening along the chest. Stuff llama firmly through opening. Stitch opening closed.
6. Embellish the ornament with pom-poms or tassels. To make tassels, refer to the illustrations on page 152. Make four small tassels with teal, green, and red floss. String tassels onto red embroidery floss and carefully remove the top tie on each tassel. Stitch the red floss ends to ornament at neck.
7. To make pom-poms, refer to the diagrams on page 152. Make two pom-poms with red and teal floss. Stitch pom-pom tails to neck and trim as desired.
8. Brush cosmetic blush onto llama cheeks below the eye.

New Year's Game Night

Gather friends to ring in the new year with a night of fun and board games. Vintage game pieces and boards play right into the theme, setting the stage for a winner of an evening.

COME ON OVER

Create playful party invitations incorporating alphabet tiles available in craft and scrapbook stores. For the background, use board-game-theme scrapbook paper. Choose a variety of tile styles to spell out FUN AND GAMES using the photo as a reference. Use double-sided tape pieces to adhere each letter to the paper. Make a photocopy for each invitation; trim to fit a blank notecard. Use glue stick to adhere a ribbon to the card as shown, followed by the photocopy. Write the invitation information inside. To duplicate this invitation graphics, the image is provided on page 157.

WINNING FAVORS

Whether enjoyed during the game night or gifted as a take-home treat, these little treasures are sure to be appreciated. Fill small, clear cellophane bags with desired treats. For each closure, twist a small screw eye into a wood game piece, such as a domino. Thread cord through the screw eye and tie around bag. Place each bag in a decorative paper snack or baking cup.

JUST FOR LOOKS

Decades old or brand new, game boards do double duty as tabletop mats. Scour thrift shops and antiques stores for colorful options. Use the boards on the snack or beverage tables.

5-4-3-2-1 HATS

Craft whimsical party hats to wear as partygoers count down to the new year. Enlarge the pattern on page 160 onto white paper; cut out. Use the pattern to cut shapes from game-theme cardstock or make photocopies of antique game boards. Bend the paper into a hat shape, overlapping at back; staple to secure. Hot-glue cord around the bottom edge. Decorate each front with a cord loop and a trio of pom-poms backed with paper flower punchouts. Glue a larger pom-pom to the hat tip.

BINGO CARD COASTERS

Vintage bingo cards make fun coasters for any size glass. Adhere the card to felt using instant adhesive. Use pinking shears to trim a narrow border. To help guests identify their beverage, use different colors of felt for each coaster.

DISTINCTLY YOURS

Antiques-store finds, game pieces like these allow you to make unique glassware charms for every guest at the party. Use an awl to poke a hole in the top edge of a wood poker chip. Twist in a tiny screw eye and leave the opening left to right as shown; add a drop of instant glue to secure. Hot-glue a game piece to the center of each poker chip. Trim around the game piece with ball chain, cut to fit using a wire cutter. Glue in place. Thread a short piece of ball-chain through the hole; fasten around glassware stem.

SURE-BET TRAY

A serving tray gets dressed for the evening with a lining of poker chips. Use hot glue to attach the chips in rows on a wood tray. Plastic chips can create a slick surface. If the tray will be carried, use wood or pressed board chips.

Merry Minis

FAMILY KEEPSAKE

A serving piece, passed down from generations, becomes a meaningful container to hold a mini artificial arrangement. Cut floral foam to fit the container. Push stems of artificial greens and pinecones into the foam. Trim with a multi-bow wreath.

SINGLE SERVING

In addition to their main purpose, holiday cups make great bases for holiday displays. Simply tuck an artificial pick or two into the cup, along with a pair of peppermint candy sticks and this little beauty is ready to shine.

GLORIOUS GROUPING

One embellished votive holder is charming but line up a trio and you have a showstopping display. Place matching holders on the ends and a larger or more ornate one in the center. Fill the vessels with artificial snowy greenery and miniature bulbs. Place a larger bulb in the center container. Dust the surface with foam snow, adding an ornament and animal statue to complete the scene.

HOLIDAY WISHES

Mouth-blown glass canisters hold seasonal sentiments from each member of the family. On small pieces of cardstock, write each family member's name. Punch a hole at one end. To attach tags to the jars, cut 10-inch lengths of cord; knot the ends. Insert the cord loop through the hole, insert the knotted ends through the loop, and pull snug. Hang tags from lid knobs. Decorate each card with nature finds, such as leaves, berries, or feathers tucked through the cord. Use raw-edge wood slices to stagger the jar heights.

MAKE A SCENE

Add some interest to a stacked candy dish. In the top tier, create a small scene with bottlebrush trees and a tiny character ornament. Use poster putty to hold the decorations in place. Sprinkle artificial snow in the bottom of the dish and put on the lid.

food

No matter how fancy or casual the gathering, when we get together with family and friends at the holidays, there must be good things to eat.

CITRUS UPSIDE-DOWN CAKE
Recipe on page 111

HAM AND EGG CUPS
Recipe on page 101

The Big Freeze

Get ahead this holiday season by making a few dishes and storing them in the freezer until needed. It's like having money in the bank!

BUTTERNUT SQUASH
MAC AND CHEESE

SPINACH-ARTICHOKE TURKEY NOODLE CASSEROLE

WHAT YOU NEED

Nonstick cooking spray

- 3 cups dry wide whole wheat egg noodles
- 1 Tbsp. canola oil
- 1 to 1¼ lb. uncooked ground turkey
- 1 medium onion, chopped
- 4 cloves garlic, minced
- 1 8-oz. pkg. cream cheese, cubed
- 1 cup chicken broth
- ⅓ cup mayonnaise
- ½ tsp. salt
- ¼ tsp. crushed red pepper
- ¼ tsp. black pepper
- 1 9-oz. pkg. frozen chopped spinach, thawed
- 1 cup chopped roasted red bell peppers
- 1 6- to 7.5-oz. jar marinated artichoke hearts, drained and cut up
- ½ cup shredded Parmesan cheese
- 1 cup crushed round rich crackers (about 24 crackers)
- 2 Tbsp. butter, melted
- 2 Tbsp. chopped fresh chives or ¼ cup chopped fresh parsley

WHAT YOU DO

1. Coat a 3-qt. baking dish or 13×9-inch disposable foil pan with cooking spray. Cook noodles according to package directions; drain.

2. In a large nonstick skillet heat oil over medium. Add turkey, onion, and garlic. Cook until turkey is browned. Remove from heat. Add cream cheese. Stir until cream cheese is melted and incorporated into turkey mixture.

3. In a large bowl whisk together next five ingredients (through black pepper). Using a double thickness of paper towels, wrap and squeeze spinach to remove some of the liquid. Add spinach, roasted red peppers, and artichoke hearts to mayonnaise mixture. Stir in turkey mixture, drained noodles, and Parmesan cheese. Spoon evenly into prepared baking dish.

4. Cover dish tightly with foil. Freeze up to 3 months.

5. To serve, preheat oven to 350°F. In a small bowl combine crushed crackers and butter. Bake frozen casserole, covered, 30 minutes. Uncover; bake 30 minutes more. Stir casserole; spread evenly in dish. Sprinkle with cracker mixture. Bake 10 to 15 minutes more or until heated through and lightly browned. Sprinkle with chives. Makes 6 servings.

To Bake Right Away Preheat oven to 350°F. Prepare as directed through Step 3. Bake, uncovered, 15 minutes. Meanwhile, in a small bowl combine crushed crackers and butter. Stir casserole; spread evenly in dish. Sprinkle with cracker mixture. Bake 10 to 15 minutes more or until heated through and lightly browned. Sprinkle with chives.

SPINACH-ARTICHOKE
TURKEY NOODLE
CASSEROLE

BUTTERNUT SQUASH MAC AND CHEESE

Photo on page 88

WHAT YOU NEED

4 cups dried rigatoni pasta (12 oz.)
1 1½-lb. butternut squash, peeled, halved lengthwise, seeded, and cut into 1-inch chunks (about 3½ cups)
2¾ cups milk
¼ cup all-purpose flour
2 cups shredded Gruyère cheese (8 oz.)
8 slices bacon
2 cups coarsely chopped sweet onions
3 oz. sourdough bread, torn
2 Tbsp. butter, melted
Cracked black pepper (optional)

WHAT YOU DO

1. Lightly butter a 3-qt. rectangular baking dish or 13×9-inch disposable foil pan. Cook pasta according to package directions; drain. Return pasta to hot pot; cover and keep warm.

2. Meanwhile, in a large saucepan combine squash and 2½ cups of the milk. Bring just to boiling over medium-high; reduce heat. Simmer, uncovered, 18 to 20 minutes or until squash is tender, stirring occasionally (watch carefully so milk doesn't bubble over). In a small bowl whisk together the remaining ¼ cup milk and the flour; stir into squash mixture. Cook and stir until thickened and bubbly. Gradually add 1½ cups of the cheese, stirring until melted.

3. In an extra-large skillet cook bacon over medium until crisp. Remove bacon; drain on paper towels, reserving 2 Tbsp. drippings in skillet. Crumble bacon. Add onions to reserved drippings. Cook, covered, over medium-low about 10 minutes or until onions are tender, stirring occasionally. Cook, uncovered, over medium-high 4 to 6 minutes or until golden, stirring frequently. Add squash mixture, bacon, and onions to cooked pasta; toss gently to combine. Transfer mixture to prepared baking dish.

4. Place bread in a food processor. Cover and pulse until coarse crumbs form (you should have about 1½ cups). Transfer to a small bowl. Drizzle with melted butter; toss to coat. Sprinkle pasta mixture with remaining ½ cup cheese and the buttered crumbs.

5. Cover dish tightly with foil. Freeze up to 1 month.

6. To serve, thaw in the refrigerator 24 hours (casserole will still be icy). Preheat oven to 350°F. Bake, covered, about 1 hour or until edges are bubbly. Let stand 5 minutes before serving. If desired, sprinkle with cracked black pepper. Makes 6 servings.

To Bake Right Away Preheat oven to 425°F. Prepare as directed through Step 4. Bake, uncovered, about 15 minutes or until edges are bubbly and top is lightly browned. Let stand 5 minutes before serving. If desired, sprinkle with cracked black pepper.

CHICKEN CORDON BLEU WILD RICE CASSEROLE

WHAT YOU NEED

Nonstick cooking spray
3 Tbsp. butter
1 8-oz. pkg. sliced fresh mushrooms
4 cloves garlic, minced
3 Tbsp. all-purpose flour
2½ cups whole milk or half-and-half
Salt and black pepper
2 8.8-oz. pouches cooked long grain and wild rice
2 cups shredded cooked chicken
1½ cups shredded Gruyère cheese (6 oz.)
1 cup chopped cooked ham
½ cup chopped green onions
1 Tbsp. butter
½ cup panko
Chopped fresh parsley

WHAT YOU DO

1. Coat a 3-qt. rectangular baking dish or 13×9-inch disposable foil pan with cooking spray. In a large skillet melt the 3 Tbsp. butter over medium. Add mushrooms and garlic; cook about 5 minutes or until tender. Stir in flour. Add milk. Cook and stir until thickened and bubbly. Season to taste with salt and pepper.

2. Stir in rice, chicken, cheese, ham, and green onions. Transfer to prepared dish.

3. Cover dish tightly with foil. Freeze up to 3 months.*

4. To serve, thaw in the refrigerator 24 hours (casserole will still be icy). Preheat oven to 350°F. Bake, covered, 30 minutes. Meanwhile, in a small bowl

CHICKEN CORDON BLEU WILD RICE CASSEROLE

melt the 1 Tbsp. butter in the microwave. Add panko. Toss to combine. Uncover dish. Sprinkle panko mixture over top. Bake about 40 minutes more or until heated through. Before serving, sprinkle with parsley and/or additional green onions. Makes 8 servings.

To Bake Right Away Preheat oven to 350°F. Prepare as directed through Step 2. In a small bowl melt 1 Tbsp. butter in the microwave. Add panko. Toss to combine. Sprinkle panko mixture over top of casserole. Bake, uncovered, about 35 minutes or until heated through. Before serving, sprinkle with parsley and/or additional green onions.

*Tip Don't lose your baking dishes and pans to the freezer. Instead, look for foil pans with a nonstick interior. These pans are designed for casseroles—even acidic recipes, like those with tomato-base sauces. If the pan comes with a domed lid, save the lid for toting—and save room in the freezer by covering the pan with plastic wrap then foil.

SPICY SAUSAGE, MUSHROOM, AND POLENTA BAKE

SPICY SAUSAGE, MUSHROOM, AND POLENTA BAKE

WHAT YOU NEED

- 1 lb. bulk Italian sausage
- 1 medium fresh jalapeño, seeded and finely chopped (optional)
- 4 cloves garlic, minced
- 1 24-oz. jar marinara sauce
- 1 Tbsp. olive oil
- 4 cups chopped fresh mushrooms
- ¾ cup thinly sliced green onions
- 1 tsp. chopped fresh rosemary
- ½ cup heavy cream
- ¼ cup dry white wine or chicken broth
- ½ tsp. salt
- 4 cups chicken broth
- ½ cup water
- 2 tsp. dried Italian seasoning, crushed
- 1½ cups cornmeal
  Nonstick cooking spray
- 2 cups shredded smoked provolone cheese (8 oz.)

WHAT YOU DO

1. In a large skillet cook sausage, jalapeño (if desired), and half of the garlic over medium-high until sausage is browned. Drain off fat. Stir in marinara sauce. Bring to boiling; reduce heat. Simmer, uncovered, 15 minutes, stirring frequently.

2. In another large skillet heat olive oil over medium. Add mushrooms, green onions, remaining garlic, and rosemary. Cook about 5 minutes or until mushrooms are tender and liquid is evaporated, stirring occasionally. Stir in cream, wine, and salt. Cook over low about 10 minutes or until thickened, stirring occasionally.

3. For polenta, in a large saucepan bring broth, water, and Italian seasoning to boiling. Slowly add cornmeal, stirring constantly. Cook and stir until mixture returns to boiling; reduce heat to low. Cook 8 to 10 minutes or until thickened, stirring occasionally.

4. Meanwhile, coat a 3-qt. rectangular baking dish or 13×9-inch disposable foil pan with cooking spray. Spread half

of the sausage mixture over bottom of prepared baking dish.

5. Working quickly, spread half of the polenta over sausage mixture in dish. Top with mushroom mixture and half of the cheese. Quickly spread remaining polenta over top as evenly as possible. Top with remaining sausage mixture and remaining cheese. Cool completely.

6. Cover dish with plastic wrap, then cover tightly with foil. Freeze up to 1 month.

7. To serve, thaw in the refrigerator overnight (casserole will still be icy). Preheat oven to 350°F. Remove plastic wrap; re-cover with foil. Bake about 1½ hours or until heated through. Let stand 10 minutes before serving. Makes 8 servings.

To Bake Right Away Preheat oven to 375°F. Prepare as directed through Step 5. Cover baking dish with a sheet of greased foil. Bake 25 to 30 minutes or until heated through. Let stand 10 minutes before serving.

PIZZA SLAB PIE

MARINATED APPLE-SAGE BRAISED PORK SHOULDER

CHICKEN IN CREAMY WINE AND MUSHROOM SAUCE

PIZZA SLAB PIE

WHAT YOU NEED

2   13.8-oz. packages refrigerated pizza dough
8   oz. bulk hot or sweet Italian sausage, cooked and drained
½   of a 10-oz. package frozen chopped spinach, thawed and squeezed dry
1   cup pizza sauce or pasta sauce
1   cup thawed and quartered frozen artichoke hearts
½   cup sliced pitted ripe olives or Kalamata olives
⅓   cup slivered red onion
2   cups shredded Italian cheese blend (8 oz.)
¾   cup shredded Parmesan cheese (3 oz.)

WHAT YOU DO

1. Preheat oven to 375°F. Lightly grease a 15×10×1-inch baking pan; set aside. Unroll one package of pizza dough on a lightly floured surface. Roll dough into a 15×10-inch rectangle. Transfer to the prepared baking pan; press edges of dough up sides of pan. Bake for 7 to 10 minutes or until light brown.
2. For filling, in a medium bowl combine sausage, spinach, pizza sauce, artichoke hearts, olives, and red onion. Spread evenly over crust in pan. Sprinkle with Italian cheese blend.
3. To freeze, cover with foil. Freeze for up to 1 month.*
4. To serve, do not thaw pizza. Preheat oven to 375°F. Bake, uncovered, for 25 minutes, covering with foil the last 5 to 10 minutes if necessary to prevent overbrowning.
5. Unroll the remaining package of pizza dough. Cut dough in long strips or random-sized pieces; place on filling. Sprinkle with Parmesan cheese.
6. Bake, uncovered, for 15 minutes more or until crust is golden and filling is heated through. Makes 12 servings.
To Bake Right Away Preheat oven to 400°F. Continue, beginning with Step 4, at baking uncovered, 25 minutes, and proceeding through Step 6.
*Tip To discourage ice crystals from forming on frozen food, let all cooked foods cool completely before wrapping or packaging to freeze.

MARINATED APPLE-SAGE BRAISED PORK SHOULDER

WHAT YOU NEED

1   2½- to 3-lb. boneless pork shoulder roast, trimmed and cut into 6 pieces Salt and black pepper
2   small onions, cut into wedges
1   Tbsp. dried sage, crushed
2   cloves garlic, minced
½   cup frozen apple juice concentrate, thawed
8   carrots, cut into 3-inch pieces
3   stalks celery, cut into 2-inch pieces Water or chicken broth
2   Tbsp. all-purpose flour Mashed potatoes (optional)

WHAT YOU DO

1. Season the pork with salt and pepper. Place meat and onions in a large resealable plastic freezer bag or container. Sprinkle sage and garlic over meat in bag. Pour apple juice concentrate over pork. Seal bag, turn to coat so marinade is equally distributed over the pork. Freeze up to 1 month.
2. To serve, let frozen bag stand at room temperature for 30 minutes. Preheat oven to 325°F. Place meat and marinade in a shallow roasting pan; add carrots and celery. Cover pan with foil. Bake for 2 to 2½ hours or until meat and vegetables are tender.
3. With a slotted spoon, transfer the pork and vegetables to a serving platter. For gravy, transfer pan drippings to a glass measuring cup. Skim off fat. Add enough water or broth to drippings to equal 1 cup. Return drippings to roasting pan. In a small bowl stir together flour and 2 Tbsp. water. Add to drippings in roasting pan. Place roasting pan on the stovetop over medium heat. Cook and stir until thickened and bubbly, scraping up any browned bits. Cook and stir 2 minutes more. Strain gravy, if desired. Serve with pork, vegetables, and, if desired, mashed potatoes. Makes 6 servings.

CHICKEN IN CREAMY WINE AND MUSHROOM SAUCE

WHAT YOU NEED

6   skinless, boneless chicken breast halves (about 2 lb.)
1   8-oz. package fresh cremini mushrooms, sliced
1   10¾-oz. can condensed golden mushroom soup
½   cup dry white wine or chicken broth
½   of an 8-oz. tub cream cheese spread with chives and onion
¼   cup butter, melted
3   cloves garlic, minced
1   0.7-oz. envelope Italian dry salad dressing mix Hot cooked rice or angel hair pasta

WHAT YOU DO

1. Place chicken breasts in a single layer in a 3-quart rectangular baking dish. Sprinkle mushrooms on chicken breasts. In a medium bowl whisk together mushroom soup, white wine, cream cheese, butter, garlic, and salad dressing mix until combined; pour over chicken.
2. Cover baking dish with plastic wrap, then foil. Freeze up to 1 month.
3. To serve, let casserole stand at room temperature for 30 minutes to thaw. Preheat oven to 350°F. Remove plastic wrap; cover with foil. Bake for 1¼ hours or until chicken is no longer pink. Remove foil; bake for 10 minutes more. Remove chicken from baking dish and place on a serving platter. Whisk sauce and spoon over chicken. Serve with hot cooked rice or pasta. Makes 6 servings.
To Bake Right Away Preheat oven to 350°F. Cover with foil and bake 30 minutes. Remove foil; bake 10 minutes more.
Tip Make your own IQF (individually quick frozen) ingredients. To keep chopped vegetables or meats from forming a clump, spread them out on a baking sheet and freeze 1 hour or until firm before packing in a freezer bag.

Food

RAVIOLI
LASAGNA WITH
CHIANTI SAUCE

RAVIOLI LASAGNA WITH CHIANTI SAUCE

WHAT YOU NEED

- 2 Tbsp. olive oil
- ½ cup chopped onion (1 medium)
- 3 cloves garlic, minced
- 1 28-oz. can crushed tomatoes
- 1 cup Chianti or other full-flavor dry red wine
- 2 tsp. dried Italian seasoning, crushed
- ¼ to ½ tsp. crushed red pepper
- 12 oz. Italian-flavor cooked chicken sausage links, halved lengthwise and sliced ½ inch thick
- 4½ cups sliced fresh cremini or button mushrooms (12 oz.)
- 1 7-oz. jar roasted red sweet peppers, drained and coarsely chopped
- ½ cup snipped fresh basil
- 2 9-oz. packages refrigerated cheese-filled ravioli
- 2 cups shredded mozzarella cheese (8 oz.)

WHAT YOU DO

1. For sauce, in a large saucepan heat 1 Tbsp. of the oil over medium heat. Add onion and garlic; cook about 3 minutes or until onion is tender, stirring occasionally. Stir in tomatoes, Chianti, Italian seasoning, and crushed red pepper. Bring to boiling; reduce heat. Simmer, uncovered, about 10 minutes or until sauce is slightly thickened.

2. Meanwhile, for the sausage layer, in an extra-large skillet heat the remaining 1 Tbsp. oil over medium heat. Add sausage and mushrooms; cook until mushrooms are tender, stirring occasionally. Stir in roasted peppers and basil.

3. To assemble lasagna, spread one-fourth of the sauce in an ungreased 3-quart rectangular baking dish. Layer with one package of the ravioli and half the sausage mixture. Spread another one-fourth of the sauce over sausage layer in dish. Sprinkle with half the cheese; spread another one-fourth of the sauce over cheese in dish. Top with remaining ravioli, sausage mixture, sauce, and cheese.

4. To freeze lasagna, cover baking dish with plastic wrap, then with foil.* Freeze up to 1 month.

ITALIAN BEEF SANDWICHES

5. To serve, thaw frozen lasagna in the refrigerator overnight (lasagna may still be a bit icy). Preheat oven to 375°F. Remove plastic wrap; cover with foil. Bake for 1 hour. Bake, uncovered, about 15 minutes more or until lasagna is heated through and cheese is bubbly. Let stand for 10 minutes before serving. Makes 8 servings.

To Bake Right Away Bake, covered, for 35 minutes in a 375°F oven. Uncover and bake, until heated through and cheese is bubbly, about 5 minutes more.

*Tip Avoid using aluminum foil to wrap dishes that contain acidic foods, such as tomatoes. Acid reacts with foil, which can give foods an off flavor. If you would like to use foil, wrap the lasagna in plastic wrap first.

ITALIAN BEEF SANDWICHES

WHAT YOU NEED

- 1 4-lb. boneless beef sirloin or rump roast, cut into 2- to 3-inch pieces
- 1 0.7-oz. envelope Italian dry salad dressing mix
- 2 tsp. dried Italian seasoning, crushed
- 1 tsp. garlic powder
- ½ to 1 tsp. crushed red pepper
- ½ cup water
- 12 hoagie rolls, split

  Roasted red sweet pepper strips (optional)
  Shredded provolone cheese (optional)

WHAT YOU DO

1. Trim fat from meat. In a large bowl combine the first five ingredients (through crushed red pepper). Place seasoned beef in a large resealable plastic freezer bag or freezer container. Freeze up to 1 month. (If using a freezer bag, lay bag flat in the freezer.)

2. To serve, let frozen seasoned beef stand at room temperature for 30 minutes. Preheat oven to 325°F. Transfer seasoned beef to a 13×9×2-inch baking pan. Drizzle with the ½ cup water. Cover with foil. Roast for 3 hours or until meat is tender. Remove meat with a slotted spoon. Using two forks, shred the meat; drizzle with some of the pan juices to moisten. Place meat on rolls. If desired, top meat with roasted red pepper strips and shredded provolone cheese. Place on a foil-lined baking sheet. Broil 4 to 5 inches from the heat for 3 to 5 minutes or until cheese is melted. Makes 12 servings.

Holiday Brunch: Go Big or Go Bite-Size

Create a holiday brunch of big-batch dishes or go for more individually-sized options.

FIRE-ROASTED TOMATO STRATA

WHAT YOU NEED
7	to 8 cups crusty bread cubes
1	to 1½ tsp. ground cumin
1	tsp. sweet paprika
⅛	to ¼ tsp. cayenne pepper
1	Tbsp. olive oil or vegetable oil
1	cup chopped onion
1	cup chopped red bell pepper
3	cloves garlic, minced
1	14.5-oz. can diced fire-roasted tomatoes, drained, reserving 2 Tbsp. of the liquid
¾	cup grape tomatoes, quartered
4	to 6 oz. crumbled feta cheese
16	eggs
3	cups milk
	Fresh cilantro sprigs

WHAT YOU DO
1. Grease a 3-qt. baking dish. Spread half of the bread cubes in prepared dish. In a small bowl stir together cumin, sweet paprika, cayenne pepper, and ½ tsp. salt.
2. In a 10-inch skillet heat oil over medium. Add next three ingredients (through garlic); cook 3 minutes or until tender. Stir in diced tomatoes and reserved liquid, grape tomatoes, and half of the spice mixture. Layer half of the tomato mixture over bread cubes. Add half of the cheese, then the remaining bread cubes, tomato mixture, and cheese.
3. In a bowl whisk together six of the eggs, the milk, and remaining spice mixture. Pour over layers, gently pressing down bread to moisten. Cover; chill 1 hour or up to 24 hours.
4. Preheat oven to 325°F. Bake, uncovered, 30 minutes. Use the back of a spoon to gently press 10 indents into strata top. Add remaining 10 eggs to indentations. Bake 25 to 30 minutes more or until a thermometer registers 170°F. Let stand 15 minutes. Top with cilantro; sprinkle with black pepper. Makes 10 servings.

BANANA-AND-NUT–BUTTER STUFFED FRENCH TOAST

WHAT YOU NEED
12	oz. ½-inch-thick slices brioche bread, halved diagonally (about 20 slices)
½	of an 8-oz. carton mascarpone cheese or whipped cream cheese
¼	cup + 1 Tbsp. nut butter
¾	cup pure maple syrup
4	bananas
4	eggs
1¾	cups milk
2	tsp. vanilla
1	tsp. ground cinnamon
2	Tbsp. butter

WHAT YOU DO
1. Grease a 2- to 2½-qt. baking dish. Arrange half of the bread slices in prepared dish; overlap slices as necessary. For filling, in a small bowl whisk together mascarpone cheese and ¼ cup each of the nut butter and maple syrup until smooth. Spoon evenly over bread in dish. Slice two of the bananas crosswise. Layer over filling. Arrange remaining bread slices on top.
2. In a large bowl whisk together eggs, milk, ¼ cup of maple syrup, vanilla, and cinnamon. Slowly pour egg mixture over bread, pressing down bread as you pour. Cover and chill 2 to 24 hours.
3. Preheat oven to 375°F. Bake, uncovered, 50 to 65 minutes or until center is set (180°F), covering with foil halfway through baking. Let stand 15 minutes.
4. Meanwhile, bias-slice remaining two bananas. In a large skillet heat butter and remaining ¼ cup maple syrup and 1 Tbsp. nut butter over medium until bubbly. Add banana slices. Cook 2 minutes or until thickened, stirring occasionally. Spoon warm banana mixture over dish. Makes 8 servings.

BANANA-AND-NUT–BUTTER STUFFED FRENCH TOAST

PLAN YOUR MENU

BIG-BATCH BRUNCH

Fire-Roasted Tomato Strata

Crisp-cooked bacon

Banana-and-Nut–Butter Stuffed
French Toast

Eggs and Bacon Dutch Baby
(recipe, page 98)

Fruit Platter with Maple-
Mascarpone Dip *(recipe, page 98)*

Apposta Cocktail *(recipe, page 98)*

**FIRE-ROASTED TOMATO
STRATA**

EGGS AND BACON DUTCH BABY

WHAT YOU NEED

5   Tbsp. butter
½   cup all-purpose flour
2   Tbsp. chopped mixed fresh herbs, such as basil, thyme, parsley, and/or oregano
½   cup milk
3   eggs
½   tsp. salt
½   tsp. black pepper
3   cups fresh spinach
3   cloves garlic, minced
¼   cup finely shredded Parmesan cheese
3   slices bacon, crisp-cooked and crumbled
2   soft-boiled eggs, peeled and halved*

WHAT YOU DO

1. Place 2 Tbsp. of the butter in a 10-inch oven-going skillet in a cold oven. Preheat oven to 425°F.
2. Meanwhile, in a medium bowl whisk together flour, 1 Tbsp. of the herbs, the milk, eggs, salt, and pepper until smooth. Chop enough of the spinach to get ½ cup; stir into batter. Pour batter into hot skillet. Bake 25 minutes or until puffed and golden.
3. Meanwhile, in an 8-inch skillet melt 1 Tbsp butter over medium. Add garlic;

cook 30 seconds. Add remaining spinach. Cook and stir 1 to 2 minutes or until wilted.
4. Remove Dutch baby from oven; sprinkle with cheese. Let stand 5 minutes (pancake will deflate during standing). In a small microwave-safe bowl melt remaining 2 Tbsp. butter; stir in remaining 1 Tbsp. herbs. Brush mixture over Dutch baby. Top with cooked spinach and bacon. Cut into wedges; top each with an egg half. Makes 4 servings.
*Tip For soft-boiled eggs, bring a saucepan of water to boiling over medium-high. Use a slotted spoon to carefully lower eggs, one at a time, into water. Cook 7 minutes, adjusting heat to maintain a gentle boil. Transfer eggs to a bowl of ice water; let stand about 2 minutes or until slightly warm.

FRUIT PLATTER WITH MAPLE-MASCARPONE DIP

WHAT YOU NEED

2   navel oranges, peeled and sliced
2   kiwifruits, peeled and cut into chunks
1   cup fresh pineapple chunks
2   apples, cored and sliced
2   pears, cored and sliced
3   Tbsp. fresh lemon juice
1   cup red and green seedless grapes
3   Tbsp. pomegranate seeds (optional)

1   8-oz. carton mascarpone cheese
¼   cup pure maple syrup

WHAT YOU DO

1. Arrange oranges, kiwifruits, pineapple, apples, and pears on a large platter; brush with 2 Tbsp. of the lemon juice.
2. Thread grapes on appetizer skewers, alternating colors. Add skewers to platter. Add pomegranate seeds (if using).
3. For dip, in a small bowl stir together mascarpone cheese, maple syrup, and remaining 1 Tbsp. lemon juice. Serve dip with fruit. Makes 8 servings.

APPOSTA COCKTAIL

WHAT YOU NEED

1   750-ml bottle gin
2   cups Aperol
2   cups sweet white vermouth
⅔   cup strained lemon juice
½   cup chilled grapefruit soda
     Thyme sprigs and orange peel, for garnish
     Ice

WHAT YOU DO

In a pitcher combine the first five ingredients (through grapefruit soda). Garnish with thyme and orange peel. Serve over ice. Makes 10 to 12 servings.

FRUIT PLATTER WITH MAPLE-MASCARPONE DIP

APPOSTA COCKTAIL

**EGGS AND BACON
DUTCH BABY**

PLAN YOUR MENU

BITE-SIZE BUFFET

Caramelized Pear Dutch Baby

Mini Bacon-Mushroom Quiches

Ham and Egg Cups

Fruit and cheese platter

Nutty Honey Mini Rolls
(recipe, page 103)

Mimosa Flight *(recipe, page 103)*

CARAMELIZED
PEAR DUTCH BABY

CARAMELIZED PEAR DUTCH BABY

WHAT YOU NEED

2   Tbsp. butter, cut up
3   Tbsp. granulated sugar
¼   tsp. ground cinnamon
¼   tsp. ground cardamom
1   cup thinly sliced cored pears
3   eggs
½   cup milk
½   cup all-purpose flour
½   tsp. vanilla
⅛   tsp. salt
⅓   cup caramel ice cream topping,
    warmed
    Powdered sugar

WHAT YOU DO

1. Place butter in a 10-inch oven-going skillet in a cold oven. Preheat oven to 425°F.
2. Meanwhile, in a bowl stir together 2 Tbsp. of the granulated sugar and ⅛ tsp. each of the cinnamon and cardamom. Add pear slices; toss gently to coat.
3. Remove skillet from oven; swirl to coat surface with butter. Spread pear mixture evenly in skillet. Bake 10 minutes or until pears are slightly softened and butter is bubbling and beginning to brown around the edges.
4. Meanwhile, in a medium bowl whisk together next five ingredients (through salt), remaining 1 Tbsp. granulated sugar, and remaining ⅛ tsp. each cinnamon and cardamom until smooth.
5. Pour batter over pears. Bake 25 minutes or until puffed and golden brown. Remove skillet; let stand 5 minutes (pancake will deflate during standing). Drizzle with caramel topping; sprinkle with powdered sugar. Cut into wedges. Makes 4 servings.

MINI BACON-MUSHROOM QUICHES

WHAT YOU NEED

    Nonstick cooking spray
½   of a 17.3-oz. pkg. frozen puff pastry
    sheets (1 sheet), thawed
4   slices bacon
1½ cups sliced fresh stemmed shiitake,
    cremini, and/or button mushrooms
¾   cup shredded Swiss cheese (3 oz.)

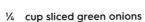

MINI BACON-MUSHROOM QUICHES

¼   cup sliced green onions
2   eggs, lightly beaten
¼   cup milk
1   8-oz. carton sour cream

WHAT YOU DO

1. Preheat oven to 400°F. Coat twelve 2½-inch muffin cups with cooking spray. On a lightly floured surface roll out pastry to a 12-inch square. Cut into twelve 4×3-inch rectangles. Press pastry rectangles onto bottoms and up sides of muffin cups. Prick bottoms with a fork. Bake 8 minutes. Remove from oven. Press centers down with the back of a teaspoon.
2. In a large skillet cook bacon until crisp; drain on paper towels and crumble. Reserve 1 Tbsp. drippings in skillet; discard remaining drippings.
3. For filling, cook mushrooms in reserved drippings until tender and liquid evaporates. In a medium bowl combine mushrooms, crumbled bacon, cheese, and green onions. Spoon filling into each pastry shell. In the same bowl whisk together remaining ingredients; spoon over filling in shells.
4. Bake 12 to 15 minutes or until set. Carefully remove from muffin cups. Serve warm. Makes 12 mini quiches.

HAM AND EGG CUPS

Photo on page 87

WHAT YOU NEED

    Nonstick cooking spray
8   thin slices deli-style cooked ham
¼   cup shredded mozzarella cheese
8   eggs
    Ground black pepper
8   tsp. basil pesto (optional)
8   cherry tomatoes or grape
    tomatoes, halved

WHAT YOU DO

1. Preheat oven to 350°F. Coat eight 2½-inch muffin cups with cooking spray. Gently press a ham slice into each prepared muffin cup, carefully ruffling edges of the ham. Divide cheese among the ham-lined muffin cups.
2. Break an egg into a measuring cup, and slip egg into a muffin cup. Repeat with the remaining eggs. Sprinkle with pepper. If desired, spoon 1 tsp. pesto onto each egg. Top with tomato halves.
3. Bake for 18 to 20 minutes or until whites are completely set and yolks are thickened. Let stand in muffin cups for 3 to 5 minutes before serving. Carefully remove egg cups from muffin cups. Makes 8 servings.

NUTTY HONEY
MINI ROLLS

MIMOSA FLIGHT

NUTTY HONEY MINI ROLLS

WHAT YOU NEED

- Nonstick cooking spray
- ¼ cup finely chopped toasted almonds
- 2 Tbsp. butter, softened
- 2 Tbsp. honey
- 1 tsp. ground cinnamon
- 1 8-oz. package refrigerated crescent dough for recipes or refrigerated crescent rolls
- 1 recipe Honey Icing (recipe follows)

WHAT YOU DO

1. Preheat oven to 375°F. Lightly coat twenty-four 1¾-inch muffin cups with nonstick cooking spray; set aside. Reserve 2 Tbsp. of the almonds. For filling, in a small bowl stir together the remaining 2 tablespoons almonds, the butter, honey, and cinnamon; set aside.

2. Unroll crescent dough and cut into two equal rectangles, or if using regular crescent roll dough, pinch together seams of dough pieces to form two equal rectangles.

3. Spread filling over dough rectangles, leaving about ¼ inch unfilled along the long sides. Starting from a long side, roll up each dough rectangle. Pinch dough to seal seams. Slice each rolled rectangle into 12 equal pieces. Place a piece, cut side up, in each prepared muffin cup.

4. Bake about 10 minutes or until golden. Cool in muffin cups for 1 minute. Carefully remove rolls from muffin cups and arrange on a serving platter; cool slightly. Drizzle warm rolls with Honey Icing. Sprinkle with the reserved 2 Tbsp. almonds. Makes 24 rolls.

Honey Icing In a small bowl stir together 1 cup powdered sugar, 2 Tbsp. honey, and 1 Tbsp. milk. If necessary, stir in additional milk, 1 tsp. at a time, to reach drizzling consistency.

MIMOSA FLIGHT

Invite your guests to sample a variety of sparkling wine-and-juice pairings in a mimosa flight. It's a tasty way to introduce new flavors and spark conversation. Include standard juices such as orange or grapefruit or surprise infusions like pear nectar and pomegranate juice. To create a mocktail flight, substitute sparkling lemon water for the champagne.

WHAT YOU NEED

- 6 Tbsp. (3 oz.) freshly squeezed orange juice
- 2 Tbsp. (1 oz.) Lillet Blanc
- 1 Tbsp. (½ oz.) dry gin
- ¼ cup (2 oz.) chilled Prosecco or sparkling wine

WHAT YOU DO

In a champagne flute, combine orange juice, Lillet, and gin. Top with Prosecco. Makes 1 serving.

Note Lillet Blanc is a French white wine that has citrus liqueur added to it. It is served chilled or used as a cocktail ingredient.

Mug Buddies

A mug of something sweet to sip served with something to nibble on is a favorite holiday treat. These drink-and-cookie combos are paired up to complement each other perfectly.

CHOCOLATE CHAI COOKIES

CHOCOLATE CHAI COOKIES

WHAT YOU NEED

2	cups all-purpose flour
⅓	cup unsweetened cocoa powder
2	Tbsp. instant chai tea mix
1	cup butter, softened
1	cup superfine sugar
¼	tsp. salt
1	oz. unsweetened chocolate, melted and cooled
1	egg
1	egg yolk
2	tsp. vanilla
	Royal Icing (recipe follows)

WHAT YOU DO

1. In a medium bowl stir together flour, cocoa powder, and chai tea mix. In a large bowl beat butter with a mixer on medium to high for 30 seconds. Add sugar and salt. Beat until combined, scraping bowl as needed. Beat in melted chocolate. Beat in egg, egg yolk, and vanilla. Add flour mixture; beat in until just combined. Divide the dough in half. Cover and chill 1 hour or until dough is easy to handle.

2. Preheat oven to 375°F. On a lightly floured surface, roll one portion of dough at a time to ⅛ inch thick. Using a 3- to 3½-inch candy cane cookie cutter, cut out dough. (If necessary, dip cutters in flour to prevent sticking.) Place cutouts 1 inch apart on ungreased cookie sheets. Make sure the crooks in the candy canes are wide enough to fit over a mug rim. Reroll scraps once.

3. Bake about 7 minutes or until edges are firm. If necessary, open crooks in candy canes. Remove; cool on a wire rack. Decorate as desired with Royal Icing. Makes 42 cookies.

Royal Icing In a large bowl, stir together 1¾ cups powdered sugar, 4½ tsp. meringue powder, ¼ tsp. cream of tartar, ¼ cup warm water, and ½ tsp. vanilla. Beat with an electric mixer on low until combined. Beat on high until mixture is very stiff, 7 to 10 minutes.

PUMPKIN EGGNOG
Recipe on page 107

**PUMPKIN COOKIES WITH
CANDIED PEPITAS**
Recipe on page 107

HOT CHOCOLATE
BOMBS

PUMPKIN EGGNOG

Photo on page 105

WHAT YOU NEED

3	cups heavy cream
2½	cups milk
12	egg yolks
1⅓	cups sugar
¾	cup canned pumpkin
2	tsp. pumpkin pie spice
2	Tbsp. vanilla
	Freshly grated nutmeg

WHAT YOU DO

1. In a large saucepan combine 1 cup each of the cream and milk, the egg yolks, and sugar. Cook and stir over medium about 5 minutes or until mixture just coats a metal spoon; do not boil. Place pan in a large bowl of ice water about 5 minutes or until slightly cool, stirring constantly.
2. Strain mixture through a fine-mesh sieve into a pitcher. Stir in the remaining 2 cups cream and 1½ cups milk, the pumpkin, pumpkin pie spice, and vanilla. Cover; chill 4 to 24 hours. Top servings with nutmeg. Makes 8 servings.

PUMPKIN COOKIES WITH CANDIED PEPITAS

Photo on page 105

WHAT YOU NEED

3½	cups all-purpose flour
3	tsp. pumpkin pie spice
½	tsp. baking soda
½	tsp. salt
1½	cups packed brown sugar
½	cup vegetable oil
1	egg
1	Tbsp. vanilla
¾	cup canned pumpkin
½	tsp. orange zest
2	8-oz. pkg. cream cheese, softened
⅔	cup powdered sugar
1	recipe Candied Pepitas (recipe follows)

WHAT YOU DO

1. In a medium bowl combine flour, 1 tsp. of the pumpkin pie spice, the baking soda, and salt. In a large bowl beat brown sugar, oil, egg, and vanilla with a mixer on medium to high until combined, scraping bowl as needed. Beat in pumpkin and orange zest until combined. Beat in flour mixture. Divide dough in half.

2. Roll each portion of dough between two sheets of parchment paper to ⅛ inch thick. Transfer to baking sheets; chill 30 minutes.
3. Preheat oven to 350°F. Remove top sheet of parchment from dough. Using 2- to 2½-inch round cookie cutters, cut out dough. Place cutouts 2 inches apart on greased cookie sheets. Reroll scraps once between sheets of parchment paper. Chill 30 minutes before cutting and baking.
4. Bake about 13 minutes or until edges are light brown. Remove; cool on a wire rack.
5. In a medium bowl beat cream cheese with a mixer on medium 30 seconds. Add powdered sugar and the remaining 2 tsp. pumpkin pie spice. Beat until light and fluffy. Spread frosting on cookies and top with Candied Pepitas. Makes 48 cookies.
Candied Pepitas In a 6-inch heavy skillet heat 2 Tbsp. granulated sugar and ⅛ tsp. salt over medium-high, shaking skillet several times to heat sugar evenly (do not stir). Heat until some of the sugar is melted and syrupy. Stir only the melted sugar to keep it from overbrowning, stirring in remaining sugar as it melts. Reduce heat to low. Cook and stir until all sugar is melted and golden. Stir in 1 tsp. butter. Add ½ cup roasted pumpkin seeds (pepitas) to skillet, stirring to coat. Transfer to greased foil. While warm, use forks to separate mixture into clusters; cool.

HOT CHOCOLATE BOMBS

WHAT YOU NEED

1	to 2 Tbsp. instant hot chocolate mix
1	to 2 Tbsp. marshmallow bits
1	to 2 Tbsp. mini chocolate chips or mint-chocolate chips
4	oz. semisweet or dark chocolate, chopped
	Melted white baking chocolate and/or sprinkles (optional)
48	oz. hot chocolate or milk

WHAT YOU DO

1. In a small bowl combine hot chocolate mix, marshmallow bits, and chocolate chips.
2. Place 3 oz. of the chopped chocolate in a small bowl. Microwave 60 seconds or until melted, stirring every 15 seconds. The temperature of the melted chocolate

should be 113°F. If necessary, microwave at 5- to 10-second intervals or until a thermometer registers 113°F. Add the remaining 1 oz. chopped chocolate. Stir vigorously about 2 minutes or until completely smooth. If small pieces of chocolate remain, microwave at 5-second intervals, stirring until smooth. The chocolate temperature should be 88°F.
3. Use a small, clean paintbrush to brush chocolate inside 1- or 2½-inch shallow silicone half-moon chocolate molds, creating a thick enough layer to coat sides completely.* Freeze 5 minutes.
4. Fill half of the chocolate shells with 1 to 2 Tbsp. marshmallow mixture. Carefully loosen and pop the remaining half of the chocolate shells from the molds. To assemble each chocolate bomb, brush edge of a filled chocolate shell (still in the mold) with some of the remaining melted chocolate; gently press edge of unfilled chocolate shell into the melted chocolate to seal. Chill 2 to 3 minutes or until set. Carefully loosen and pop the assembled bombs from the molds.
5. If you like, decorate assembled bombs. Place melted white chocolate in a resealable plastic bag. Snip a small hole in one corner and drizzle over seams in bombs. Add sprinkles. Freeze 5 minutes. Transfer bombs to a storage container. Store at room temperature up to 2 weeks.
6. To serve, place one bomb in a small mug for small bombs and a large mug for large bombs. Slowly pour 4 to 6 oz. heated hot chocolate or milk over the bomb; stir. Makes 12 small bombs or 3 large bombs.
***Tip** The chocolate will set quickly in the molds. It's OK to go back and paint over the chocolate that has set to ensure the molds are completely covered. Make a few at a time to see what amount of chocolate works best with your mold. Or brush a layer of chocolate, chill, and brush again.

Sunny Citrus

Fresh, juicy citrus—grapefruits, oranges, lemons, clementines, and kumquats—are at peak season in the winter, bringing a ray of sunshine to the holiday table.

CLEMENTINE-
ROASTED CHICKEN

CLEMENTINE-ROASTED CHICKEN

WHAT YOU NEED

- 7 clementines or desired oranges
- 1 3½- to 4-lb. whole broiler-fryer chicken
- 1 tsp. kosher salt
- ½ tsp. freshly cracked black pepper
- 4 strips bacon
- 12 fresh sage leaves
- ⅓ cup maple syrup
- ¼ cup dry sherry
- 1 Tbsp. extra virgin olive oil
- 3 cloves garlic, minced

WHAT YOU DO

1. Preheat oven to 450°F. Halve clementines. Thinly slice four of the halves.
2. Season inside and outside of chicken with salt and pepper. Place one clementine half in cavity. Twist wing tips under back; tie legs to tail using 100%-cotton kitchen string. Place chicken, breast side up, in a 13×9-inch baking pan.
3. Lay bacon strips lengthwise on chicken breast; tuck six sage leaves and the clementine slices under bacon.
4. For vinaigrette, juice four of the clementine halves into a small bowl. Whisk in maple syrup, sherry, oil, and garlic.
5. Place remaining five clementine halves around chicken. Chop remaining sage leaves; sprinkle over clementines. Roast chicken 20 minutes. Spoon half of the vinaigrette over chicken. Reduce heat to 350°F; cover chicken with foil. Roast 50 to 60 minutes, spooning remaining vinaigrette over chicken every 15 minutes. Remove foil. Roast 10 minutes more or until chicken is done (at least 170°F in thigh). Cover with foil; let stand 10 minutes.
6. To serve, squeeze one roasted clementine half over chicken. Makes 4 servings.

SALMON WITH KUMQUATS

WHAT YOU NEED

- 2½ cups kumquats, halved
- 2 Tbsp. sea salt
- 4 6-oz. salmon fillets, skin on
- 1 large navel orange
- 2 cups water
- 5 Tbsp. extra virgin olive oil
- ½ cup thinly sliced shallots
- 2 tsp. prepared horseradish
- 2 tsp. packed brown sugar
- ⅔ cup dry white wine
- ¼ cup fresh basil leaves, thinly sliced
- ½ of a head radicchio, shredded

WHAT YOU DO

1. In a medium bowl sprinkle kumquat halves with 1 Tbsp. of the sea salt; let stand 25 minutes. Rinse under cold water; drain and pat dry.
2. Meanwhile, to brine salmon, place fillets in a shallow dish. Zest and juice orange over a bowl; stir in the water and remaining 1 Tbsp. sea salt until dissolved. Pour brine over salmon; let stand at room temperature 15 minutes.
3. In a 12-inch nonstick skillet heat 3 Tbsp. of the oil over medium. Add kumquats and shallots. Cook 8 minutes or until starting to brown, stirring occasionally. Transfer to a small bowl. Wipe skillet clean.
4. Remove salmon from brine; pat dry. Season with additional sea salt and black pepper. In same skillet add remaining 2 Tbsp. oil; heat 1 to 2 minutes over medium. Add salmon, skin side down (oil will sizzle). Press with a spatula to keep skin from curling. Cook 8 minutes or until skin is browned and crispy and fillet is opaque. Use tongs to carefully turn fillets over; sear 1 minute. Transfer salmon to a cutting board. Tent with foil.
5. Drain fat from skillet. Heat skillet over medium-high. Add kumquat mixture, horseradish, and brown sugar; cook 1 minute. Add wine; cook 2 to 3 minutes or until mixture reaches saucelike consistency. Remove from heat. Stir in half of the basil.
6. Serve salmon over shredded kumquat mixture and radicchio. Top with remaining basil. Makes 4 servings.

SALMON WITH KUMQUATS

ORANGE-
COUSCOUS
SALAD

ORANGE-COUSCOUS SALAD

WHAT YOU NEED

- 6 large Cara Cara, navel, or other oranges
- 4 Tbsp. extra virgin olive oil
- 1 cup Israeli couscous
- 1¼ cups reduced-sodium chicken broth or vegetable broth
- 3 cloves garlic, minced
- 1 Tbsp. chopped fresh thyme
- 1 cup very thinly sliced red onion
- ¼ cup blanched hazelnuts, toasted and coarsely chopped*
- ¼ cup coarsely chopped pitted Castelvetrano olives or Manzanilla olives
- 2 Tbsp. red wine vinegar
- ¼ tsp. coarse salt
- ⅛ tsp. freshly cracked black pepper
  Crushed red pepper (optional)

WHAT YOU DO

1. Use a vegetable peeler to carefully remove strips of zest from one orange, avoiding the white pith.

2. In a medium saucepan heat 1 Tbsp. oil over medium. Add couscous; cook and stir 2 minutes or until lightly toasted. Add two of the orange strips, the broth, and ¼ tsp. salt. Bring to boiling; reduce heat. Cook, covered, 12 to 15 minutes or until couscous is tender and liquid is absorbed. Let cool; discard orange strips.

3. Meanwhile, use a paring knife to remove peel and pith from remaining oranges. Working over a small bowl to catch juices, cut out each segment from membranes. (Or slice oranges crosswise into wheels.)

4. To make citrus oil, chop enough of the remaining orange strips to get 1 Tbsp. In a 10-inch skillet combine chopped strips, remaining 3 Tbsp. oil, the garlic, and thyme. Heat over low 5 minutes or until warm.

5. On a serving platter combine orange segments and juice, couscous, red onion, hazelnuts, and olives. Drizzle with red wine vinegar. Spoon citrus oil over top. Sprinkle with salt and black pepper and, if using, crushed red pepper. Makes 6 servings.

*Tip To toast, spread hazelnuts evenly in a shallow pan. Bake in a 350°F oven 5 to 10 minutes, stirring twice (watch closely).

CITRUS UPSIDE-DOWN CAKE

CITRUS UPSIDE-DOWN CAKE

WHAT YOU NEED

- ¾ cup + ⅔ cup sugar
- 1 lb. unpeeled citrus fruit (oranges, blood oranges, and/or Meyer lemons), thinly sliced and seeds removed
- 1 cup all-purpose flour
- ¼ tsp. baking soda
- ¼ tsp. salt
- ⅓ cup butter, softened
- 1 egg
- 1 egg yolk
- 1 tsp. vanilla
- 1 tsp. orange zest
- ½ of an 8-oz. carton sour cream
  Whipped cream (optional)

WHAT YOU DO

1. Grease a 9-inch round baking pan. In a large skillet stir together ¾ cup of the sugar and ¼ cup water. Bring just to boiling; stir to dissolve sugar. Add citrus slices. Simmer, uncovered, 10 minutes, stirring occasionally. Remove from heat. Transfer slices to prepared pan, overlapping to fit. Reserve syrup in skillet.

2. Preheat oven to 350°F. In a medium bowl stir together next three ingredients (through salt).

3. In a large bowl beat butter with a mixer on medium 30 seconds. Beat in remaining ⅔ cup sugar until combined. Add egg and yolk, beating well after each. Beat in ½ tsp. of the vanilla and the orange zest until combined. Alternately add flour mixture and sour cream, beating just until combined after each addition. Spread batter over citrus in pan.

4. Bake 30 to 35 minutes or until golden and a toothpick comes out clean. Cool on a wire rack 20 minutes.

5. Loosen cake from sides of pan. Invert onto a large platter. Stir remaining ½ tsp. vanilla into reserved syrup. Slice cake with a serrated knife. Serve warm with syrup. If you like, top with whipped cream and additional orange zest. Makes 8 servings.

MEYER LEMON RICOTTA COOKIES

WHAT YOU NEED

- ½ cup butter, softened
- 1 cup sugar
- 1 tsp. baking soda
- ½ tsp. poppy seeds
- ¼ tsp. salt
- 1 egg
- 1 cup whole milk ricotta cheese
- 2 tsp. Meyer lemon zest
- 1 tsp. vanilla
- 1¾ cups all-purpose flour
- 1 recipe Meyer Lemon Glaze (recipe follows)

WHAT YOU DO

1. Preheat oven to 350°F. Line two cookie sheets with parchment paper. In a large bowl beat butter with a mixer on medium 30 seconds. Add next four ingredients (through salt). Beat until combined, scraping bowl as needed. Beat in next four ingredients (through vanilla) until combined. Beat in flour.

2. Drop dough by rounded scoops (2 tsp.) 2 inches apart onto prepared cookie sheets. Bake 10 to 12 minutes or until cookies appear set and bottoms are lightly browned. Cool on cookie sheets 2 minutes. Remove; cool on wire racks.

3. Dip cookies into Meyer Lemon Glaze, allowing excess to drip off. If you like, sprinkle with additional lemon zest. Let stand 30 minutes or until set. Makes 40 cookies.

Meyer Lemon Glaze In a small bowl stir together 1½ cups powdered sugar, ½ tsp. Meyer lemon zest, 2 Tbsp. Meyer lemon juice, 1 Tbsp. light-color corn syrup, and a pinch of salt. If necessary, stir in additional Meyer lemon juice, 1 tsp. at a time, to reach glazing consistency.

Cup-a-tizers!

These delicious dip and dipper combos keep snacking easy.

CHARCUTERIE CUP-A-TIZER

WHAT YOU DO

Add dried apricots and nuts, such as cashews or pecans, to cups. Fill with cut-up cheese, such as sharp cheddar, Gruyère, or Brie; sliced pepperoni, salami, or prosciutto; grape clusters or apple slices; and bread or crackers, such as sliced French baguette bread or wheat crackers. Add a cornichon.

GYRO CUP-A-TIZER

WHAT YOU DO

Cook Italian-flavor chicken sausage according to package directions. Cool 15 minutes, then cut into pieces. Spoon purchased tzatziki sauce into cups. Add cucumber spears, cherry or grape tomatoes, halved mini bell peppers, chicken sausage, pita chips, and, if you like, black olives.

CRAB RANGOON CUP-A-TIZER

WHAT YOU DO

Preheat oven to 400°F. For wonton chips, halve wonton wrappers diagonally. Place on parchment paper-lined baking sheets. Lightly brush wrappers with olive oil; sprinkle with garlic salt. Bake 8 to 10 minutes or until crisp. In a bowl beat one 8-oz. pkg. cream cheese, softened; one 5-oz. can crabmeat, well drained; ¼ cup sour cream; ¼ cup sliced green onions; ¼ tsp. garlic powder; and ⅛ tsp. cayenne pepper with a mixer until combined. Spoon dip into cups; top with Thai chile sauce. Add wonton chips and sugar snap peas. Makes 1½ cups dip.

CHOCOLATE MOUSSE CUP-A-TIZER

WHAT YOU DO

In a medium bowl beat one 8-oz. pkg. cream cheese, softened, and one 7-oz. jar marshmallow creme with a mixer until smooth. Gradually beat in ¼ cup unsweetened cocoa powder and 1 tsp. vanilla. Fold in ¾ cup thawed frozen whipped dessert topping. Spoon dip into cups. Add fresh berries, cubed angel food cake, pretzels, and/or graham crackers for dipping. Makes 2 cups dip.

gifts

SHARE YOUR TALENTS
Make the holidays memorable
for family and friends.

Food Gifts

Spread holiday cheer with homemade cookies, candy, fruit cordial, treats for the pup—and more—wrapped with love and creativity.

FANCIFUL PEPPERMINT FUDGE

EASY AS 1-2-3

With just a few simple steps, you can put together a slew of gifting plates in a hurry. Tie a bow from ¼-inch ribbon; hot-glue to lower righthand corner of paper plate. Press holiday stickers on each side of the bow. Detail the design by hot-gluing semicircle trims in the center of the bow and integrated with the stickers. Place the fudge on the plate. Slip the plate into a cellophane bag and close with a twist tie.

FANCIFUL PEPPERMINT FUDGE

WHAT YOU NEED

4   cups granulated sugar
2   5-oz. can evaporated milk (1⅓ cups total)
1   cup butter
1   12-oz. package semisweet chocolate pieces (2 cups)
1   7-oz. jar marshmallow creme
½   tsp. peppermint extract
¾   cup coarsely broken peppermint candies* (optional)

WHAT YOU DO

1. Line a 13×9×2-inch pan with foil, extending foil over edges of pan. Butter foil and set pan aside.
2. Butter the sides of a heavy 3-quart saucepan. In the saucepan, combine the sugar, evaporated milk, and butter. Cook and stir over medium-high heat until mixture boils. Reduce heat to medium; continue cooking and stirring 10 minutes.
3. Remove pan from heat. Add chocolate pieces, the marshmallow creme, and peppermint extract. Stir until chocolate melts and mixture is combined. Beat by hand for 1 minute. Spread into prepared pan. Sprinkle with peppermint candies, if you like. Score into 1-inch pieces while warm. Cover and chill.
4. When fudge is firm, use foil to lift it out of pan. Cut into squares. Store in tightly covered container in the refrigerator. Makes 96 squares.
*Tip For a neater appearance, shake the peppermint pieces in a sieve to remove the very small pieces.

ZESTY POPCORN SNACK MIX

ZESTY POPCORN SNACK MIX

WHAT YOU NEED

6   cups unsalted popped popcorn or broken unsalted rice cakes*
3   cups corn chips or coarsely broken tortilla chips
3   cups mini pretzel twists
1½   cups dry-roasted cashews or peanuts
¼   cup butter, melted
2   Tbsp. Worcestershire sauce
1   Tbsp. chili powder
2   tsp. ground cumin
1   tsp. garlic salt
½   tsp. cayenne pepper
½   cup snipped dried apricots

WHAT YOU DO

1. In a large roasting pan combine popcorn, corn chips, pretzel twists, and cashews. In a small bowl combine butter, Worcestershire sauce, chili powder, cumin, garlic salt, and cayenne pepper. Pour the butter mixture over the snack mix, tossing until evenly combined.
2. Bake in a 250°F oven for 30 minutes or until the coating on snack mix begins to darken slightly, stirring occasionally.
3. Spread mixture onto a large piece of foil to cool. Stir in dried apricots. Store mixture in an airtight container for up to 2 days.* Makes 18 servings.
*Tip For longer storage, use rice cakes.

JINGLE ALL THE WAY

Spread holiday cheer with heaping handfuls of delicious snack mix, packaged in festive popcorn tubs. To make the embellishment, tie two ¼-inch-wide ribbons into a bow. Hot-glue the bow to the upper right corner of the tub front. Hot-glue three small jingle bells in the bow's center. Line the popcorn tub with a cellophane bag, fill with mix, and close with a twist tie.

BLACK CURRANT CORDIAL

BLACK CURRANT CORDIAL

WHAT YOU NEED
1   cup vodka or gin
1½ cups sugar
2   cups fresh or frozen black currants

WHAT YOU DO
1. In a medium saucepan heat the vodka or gin over medium heat to 110°F. Remove saucepan from heat.

2. In a 1-qt. glass or ceramic container stir together warm vodka or gin and sugar. Stir until sugar dissolves. Stir in black currants. Cover. Let stand in a cool dark place for 1 week.

3. Line a sieve with several layers of 100% cotton cheesecloth. Set sieve over a large bowl. Strain cordial through sieve. Transfer strained cordial to a bottle and currants to a pint jar. Seal and label. Store in the refrigerator for up to 1 month. Serve cordial with club soda and a squeeze of lime or use cordial and currants as a topping for cakes and sundaes. Makes 1⅔ cups cordial and 1½ cups currants.

CHOCOLATE RUM TRUFFLES

WHAT YOU NEED
6   oz. semisweet chocolate, coarsely chopped
¼   cup butter
3   Tbsp. whipping cream
1   beaten egg yolk
3   tsp. rum, brandy, or whipping cream
1   lb. chocolate-flavored candy coating, chopped
    Vanilla-flavored or pink or green candy coating, melted, for decorating (optional)
    Finely chopped marcona almonds (optional)

WHAT YOU DO
1. Combine chocolate, butter, and the 3 Tbsp. whipping cream in a heavy 2-quart saucepan. Cook over low heat, stirring constantly, until chocolate is melted (about 10 minutes). Remove saucepan from heat.

2. Gradually stir about half of the hot mixture into the beaten egg yolk. Return egg mixture to saucepan. Cook over medium heat, stirring constantly, about 2 minutes or until slightly thickened. Remove saucepan from heat.

3. Stir in rum, brandy, or whipping cream. Transfer chocolate mixture to a small mixing bowl. Chill about 1 hour or until mixture is room temperature and smooth, stirring occasionally.

4. Beat the cooled chocolate mixture with an electric mixer on medium speed about 2 minutes or until slightly fluffy. Chill about 15 minutes or until mixture holds its shape. Drop mixture

GLAD TIDINGS
Give this delicious duo the adornment they deserve—festive findings in snowy white and sparkling silver. Line the jar lid with white card stock. Hot-glue snippets from a white and silver holiday pick to the bottle front and jar top. Finish with narrow ribbon bows glued to each vessel.

CHOCOLATE RUM TRUFFLES

from a rounded teaspoon onto a baking sheet lined with parchment or waxed paper. Chill about 30 minutes more or until firm. Shape into smooth balls with hands, working quickly so the truffles don't get too soft.

5. Bring water to boiling in the bottom of a double boiler or a saucepan. Remove from heat. Place chopped chocolate-flavored candy coating in top of double boiler or in a heatproof bowl and set over the boiling water, making sure the bottom of the top pan is not touching the water. Stir frequently until coating melts. Or, melt coating in the microwave oven: In a 2½-quart microwave-safe bowl, microwave candy coating on 100% power (high) for 2 minutes. Stir. If necessary, microwave 30 seconds more or until almost melted. Coating may not look melted until stirred.

6. Drop truffles, one at a time, into melted candy coating; turn truffles with a large, long-tine fork to coat. Lift truffle out with the fork without piercing the centers; draw fork across rim of pan to remove excess coating. Invert truffles onto a parchment or waxed paper-lined baking sheet. If desired, twist fork slightly as candy falls to make a swirl on top.

7. Let dipped truffles dry until candy coating hardens. If the candy coating becomes too thick while dipping, reheat it in the microwave. Or, for coating that's been melted in a double boiler, replace the cooled water with warm water. Stir coating constantly until it once again reaches dipping consistency.

8. To decorate truffles, if desired, place melted vanilla-flavored or pink candy coating in a small, self-sealing plastic bag with a corner snipped off (opening should be very small) or a pastry bag fitted with a small, round tip. Pipe coating in a design atop truffles. Or, drizzle coating over truffles with a spoon. Let dry. Or, if desired, after chilling the shaped truffles for 30 minutes, roll them in finely chopped nuts instead of dipping them into melted chocolate. Makes about 30 truffles.
Make Ahead Tip Store truffles, tightly covered, in a cool, dry place for up to 2 weeks.

UNDER GLASS

Wash and dry a clear 10-inch glass plate. For the background, use two designs of patterned tissue paper or single layers gently separated from a paper napkin. For the stripe, cut a 1-inch strip from the darker paper. Use a paintbrush to brush decoupage medium onto the back of the plate where the strip will be placed. Carefully lay strip onto decoupage medium, smoothing with paintbrush. Next, cover the entire back of plate with decoupage medium and lay the lighter piece on top. Paint on an additional coat of decoupage medium; let dry. Trim off excess paper with pinking shears.

CRANBERRY-PISTACHIO BISCOTTI

PRETTY AS A POINSETTIA

Cut a 10×5½ piece of white corrugated paper. Cut a 10×4½-inch piece from holiday patterned paper. Center the holiday paper on the white paper; staple at short ends. Cut a 4½×1-inch strip from white card stock. Cut a 4½×1¼-inch piece from solid color paper to coordinate with holiday paper. Trim one long edge with pinking shears. Layer the colored paper on top of the white card stock with the pinked edge ¼ inch from the edge; use glue stick to adhere. Fold the colored paper around the edge of the white paper; glue in place. Glue the paper strip to the center of the band. Shape into a tube,

overlapping ends; staple to secure. To make the poinsettia, use 4 or 5 clean pistachio shells broken in half. Use hot glue to attach five shell halves in a flower formation. Add three or more on top to resemble petals. Paint the shells red, accenting with white and yellow for the center; let dry. Punch out a 1½-inch circle from white card stock. Glue to metallic gold paper; trim around circle with pinking shears. Hot-glue the poinsettia to the center of the circle, then to the center of the paper strip. Wrap biscotti in clear cellophane; tie at ends. Slip bag into the band, taping on the back to secure if needed.

CRANBERRY-PISTACHIO BISCOTTI

WHAT YOU NEED

2¾ cups all-purpose flour
1½ cups sugar
1½ tsp. baking powder
1 tsp. salt
2 eggs, lightly beaten
2 egg yolks, lightly beaten
6 Tbsp. butter, melted
¼ cup almond liqueur
1½ cups coarsely chopped pistachio nuts
1 cup coarsely chopped dried cranberries
6 oz. melted white baking chocolate with cocoa butter (optional)

WHAT YOU DO

1. Preheat oven to 325°F. Line two large cookie sheets with parchment paper.
2. In a large bowl stir together flour, sugar, baking powder, and salt. Make a well in center of flour mixture. In a small bowl combine eggs, egg yolks, melted butter, and liqueur. Add egg mixture all at once to flour mixture; stir until dough starts to form a ball. Stir in pistachios and cranberries (dough will be crumbly). Using your hands, knead dough until it comes together.
3. Turn dough out onto a lightly floured surface. Divide dough into three portions. Shape each portion into a 12-inch roll. Place two rolls 3 inches apart on one of the prepared cookie sheets. Place remaining roll on remaining cookie sheet; flatten rolls slightly to about 2 inches wide.
4. Bake on separate oven racks 25 to 30 minutes or until rolls are firm and light brown, rotating sheets halfway through. Cool cookie sheets on wire racks 15 minutes.
5. Transfer rolls to a cutting board. Using a serrated knife, cut rolls diagonally into ½-inch slices. Place slices, cut sides down, on cookie sheets.
6. Bake 10 to 12 minutes. Turn slices over; bake 10 to 12 minutes more or until light brown. Remove; cool on wire racks. (Biscotti will continue to crisp as they cool.) If desired, dip bottoms of cookies in melted white chocolate and sprinkle with additional pistachios. Chill 15 to 20 minutes or until set. Makes 48 cookies.
To Store Layer cookies between waxed paper in an airtight container. Store at room temperature up to 3 days.

CRANBERRY-PEAR FREEZER JAM

WHAT YOU NEED

4 ripe medium fresh pears, peeled, cored, and chopped (4 cups)
1 cup fresh cranberries
1 cup honey
1 Tbsp. lemon juice
½ tsp. ground ginger
¼ tsp. ground cinnamon

WHAT YOU DO

1. In a medium saucepan combine pears, cranberries, and honey. Bring to a boil over medium-high heat; reduce heat. Simmer, uncovered, stirring occasionally and using a wooden spoon to gently crush the cranberries against the side of the saucepan. Cook 10 to 20 minutes or until slightly thickened* (mixture will thicken more as it cools).
2. Stir in lemon juice, ginger, and cinnamon. Remove from heat; cool about 2 hours or until room temperature.
3. Ladle into three half-pint freezer containers, leaving a ½-inch headspace. Seal; label. Let stand at room temperature for 24 hours. Store for up to 3 weeks in the refrigerator or for up to 1 year in the freezer. Makes 3 half-pints.
*Tip To check if your jam is cooked enough, remove saucepan from heat. Place a teaspoon of the jam on a small baking sheet or plate. Place in the freezer for a minute or two. The jam should be slightly set with no free juices running from it.

WHAT A PEAR

Give your jam a jolly delivery in a jar as special as the recipe itself. To trim the lid, cut a paper circle from decorative paper that is ¼ inch smaller than lid. Use hot glue to adhere. For the pear, you may find miniature faux renditions in crafts stores. Or, do as was done here, and paint a mini pear-shaped gourd to resemble the real thing; let dry. Hot-glue the fruit to the center of the jar lid. Add a narrow ribbon adornment aside the pear.

CRANBERRY-PEAR FREEZER JAM

GRAIN-FREE
DOG TREATS

PET LOVE

Transform a cardboard box into a merry disguise for puppy treats. (Note: The box shown is 3"×7"×6½".) Measure and mark each side wall where desired; score. Mark the front and back of the doghouse peaks 1½ inches taller than the side walls. Cut each peak from the point to the sidewall score. Fold each side wall toward the center, following the peak lines. Mark where the peaks intersect; score each roof piece front to back. Cut off roof pieces ¾ inches above score line. Wrap the bottom of the doghouse with decorative paper. Cut paper rectangles for each side of the roof, adding an inch to the top and bottom and ½ inch to the length. Fold under 1 inch on each roof paper; slip the folded edge over the cardboard,

secure with tape on the inside of the box. Use double-sided tape to adhere paper to the bottom edge of the roof piece, allowing a 1-inch overhang. Use the patterns on page 158 to cut the doorway and banner from desired colors of card stock. Use glue stick to adhere the door to one end. Hot-glue silver chenille stem around the door shape. Use marking pen to draw a border on the banner. Write the dog's name in the center. Glue the banner to bend over the center of the door as shown. Use a small paper punch to make a pair of holes, ¾ inches apart, at the top center of each roof piece. Place treats inside the box. Thread bakers' string through the holes in the roof pieces, tie closed.

GRAIN-FREE DOG TREATS

WHAT YOU NEED
- ¾ cup almond flour
- ¾ cup coconut flour
- 3 ripe bananas, mashed
- ⅓ cup natural creamy peanut butter*
- 3 Tbsp. hemp or chia seeds (optional)

WHAT YOU DO
1. Preheat oven to 325°F. In a small bowl stir together the almond and coconut flours. In a medium bowl stir together mashed bananas and peanut butter until smooth. Add half of the flour and hemp seeds (if using); stir to combine. Add remaining flour and, using hands if needed, mix into a dough. Cover and chill dough for 20 minutes.

2. On a well-floured surface, roll out dough to ¼-inch thick. Using a small bone-shaped cookie cutter or knife, cut out shapes as desired. Reroll scraps as needed. Arrange shapes on parchment-lined baking sheets. Using a fork, poke 4 holes in the center of each treat.

3. Bake treats for about 25 minutes or until dried and bottoms are golden. Turn off oven and allow treats to cool inside 1 hour.** Transfer treats to a wire rack and cool completely before storing. Makes 75 small treats.

*Tip Do not select items that contain the ingredient xylitol. Xylitol is a sweetener that is sometimes found in peanut butter and yogurt products. It can be very toxic to pets, even in small amounts.

**Tip While cooling the treats in the oven isn't a necessary step, we find that this technique results in crispier treats that store a bit longer.

To Store Transfer completely cooled treats to an airtight container or resealable bag. Store at room temperature up to 2 weeks or freeze up to 3 months. Thaw before serving.

ROASTED GARLIC AND STOUT BREAD

WHAT YOU NEED
- 1 cup stout or other dark beer
- ½ cup bread flour
- 2 tsp. instant yeast
- 1 tsp. packed brown sugar
- 1 bulb garlic
- ½ tsp. olive oil
- 1½ cups bread flour
- 1 cup whole wheat flour

ROASTED GARLIC AND STOUT BREAD

- 2 Tbsp. packed brown sugar
- 1 Tbsp. shortening
- ¾ tsp. salt
   Yellow cornmeal
   1 egg, beaten with ⅓ cup water

WHAT YOU DO
1. In a medium bowl stir together the beer, bread flour, yeast, and brown sugar. Cover with plastic wrap. Let stand at room temperature (70°F to 80°F) 12 to 24 hours, stirring two or three times.

2. Preheat oven to 425°F. Peel away the dry outer layers of skin from the bulb of garlic, leaving skins and cloves intact. Cut off the pointed top portion (about ¼ inch), leaving bulb intact but exposing the individual cloves. Place garlic bulb, cut side up, in a custard cup. Drizzle with olive oil. Cover cup with foil and roast 25 minutes or until cloves feel soft when pressed. Set aside just until cool enough to handle. Squeeze out the garlic paste from individual cloves and place in a small bowl. Mash with a fork. Measure 1 Tbsp. roasted garlic (chill the remaining for another use). Cover and chill until ready to use.

3. Add the starter mixture, 1 Tbsp. roasted garlic, and the next six ingredients (through salt) to bowl. Mix well. On a lightly floured surface, knead moderately soft dough. Shape into a ball. Cover and let rest 30 minutes.

4. Reshape into a ball and place on a lightly greased or parchment-lined baking sheet sprinkled with cornmeal. Flatten slightly into a 7-inch round loaf. Using a sharp knife, make several cuts ¼ inch deep across the top of loaf.

5. Cover and let rise in a warm place 30 to 40 minutes or until nearly double. Brush with the egg wash. Bake in a 400°F oven 20 to 25 minutes or until bread sounds hollow when lightly tapped. Remove from baking sheet; cool on a wire rack. Makes 8 servings.

SNOWFLAKE DOILY
A handmade paper doily, cut snowflake style, creates a festive liner for a holiday plate charger. To make the doily, trace around the plate charger onto white parchment paper; cut out. Aligning edges, fold paper circle in half. Repeat three more times, creating a pie shape. Holding the layers firmly together, cut holly designs, or other holiday motifs, into the outer half section while leaving the center portion uncut. Use a paper punch to make small holes. Carefully unfold the paper and press with a dry iron. Place a small piece of double-sided tape in the center of the charger; center doily and press onto tape. Place the bread on the doily and wrap in cellophane before gifting.

SPICED TOMATO-MUSHROOM BLEND

WHAT YOU NEED

1   cup dried tomatoes (not oil-packed)
1   oz. dried mushrooms (shiitake, oyster, or morel)*
¼   cup dried minced onion
2   Tbsp. salt
1   Tbsp. dried thyme
1   Tbsp. cumin seed
2   tsp. crushed red pepper
1   tsp. garlic powder
1   tsp. ground cinnamon
1   tsp. ground cumin
1   tsp. ground cardamom
½   tsp. ground black pepper

WHAT YOU DO

In large bowl combine all ingredients. Place the mixture, one-fourth at a time, in blender. Cover and blend 30 seconds or until tomatoes are finely chopped.

Transfer to storage container. Refrigerate; use seasoning blend within 1 month. Makes 2 cups.

*Tip To remove grit from dried mushrooms, place in sieve and rinse under cold running water. Drain and pat dry. Place on baking sheet. Bake at 350°F for 10 minutes or until dry and crisp.

INGREDIENT INSPIRATION

Even beginners can craft this clay jar topper that's sure to be saved even after the delicious blend is gone. Cover work surface with waxed paper. Use a rolling pin to flatten green clay until ⅛-inch thick. Lightly press jar lid into clay; remove. Pick up flattened clay and trim around circle with pinking shears. Roll a small piece of green clay into a rope; repeat with white clay. Twist the two ropes together, then roll until rope is long enough to fit just inside the green clay circle. Place rope on green circle, cut off excess, and press gently to adhere together. Place the clay piece on a baking tray. Using about ½ pea-sized pieces of green and white rope, roll three small clay balls; flatten slightly and set aside. To make mushrooms, shape two small stems, one slightly larger than the other. Create a cap for the larger stem with red clay and use green for the smaller stem. Gently press onto stems. Roll tiny green clay balls and press onto the red mushroom cap. Use red clay for the polka dots on the green cap. Use a click ballpoint pen, open and closed, to make additional circles and dots on the red cap. Gently press the stems onto the green clay circle, adding the flattened circles. Roll three pea-sized balls from red clay; press onto the green base, overlapping the rope edging. Following manufacturer's instructions, bake the clay piece. Remove from oven when done; let cool. Use instant glue to adhere the clay motif to the jar lid. Should any of the pieces come loose while baking, glue them back in place. Fill the jar with blend and replace the lid. Tie a ribbon bow around the side of the lid.

PUMPKIN-GINGER SOUP

WHAT YOU NEED

1   15-oz. can pumpkin
1   14.5-oz. can vegetable broth
1½   cups mango or apricot nectar
1   Tbsp. grated fresh ginger
2   cloves garlic, minced
⅔   cup canned unsweetened coconut milk
¼   cup creamy peanut butter
2   Tbsp. rice vinegar
     Dash hot sauce or ¼ tsp. crushed red pepper
¼   cup chopped fresh cilantro
     Plain whole milk yogurt (optional)

WHAT YOU DO

1. In a large saucepan combine first five ingredients (through garlic). Bring to boiling; reduce heat. Simmer, uncovered, 30 minutes, stirring occasionally.
2. Whisk in next four ingredients (through hot sauce) until smooth. Stir in cilantro. If desired, top servings with yogurt. Makes 3 pints.

To Store Transfer to an airtight container and refrigerate up to 3 days. To reheat, cook and stir over medium heat until heated through.

SPICED TOMATO-MUSHROOM BLEND

PUMPKIN-GINGER
SOUP

THANKS TO NATURE

A pint jar holds two servings of this delicious soup. Add a few trims and this thoughtful gift is ready to deliver. To trim the jar, cut two pieces of ¼-inch-wide ribbon to encircle jar. Leaving a ¼-inch space between the ribbons, hot-glue the center of each ribbon to the jar. Working one ribbon at a time, wrap the ribbon ends to the back; tack with hot glue. For the star attraction, glue a small artificial greenery stem, pinecone, and berries to the jar front. Brush the tops of the trims with white acrylic paint; let dry.

Sewing Snippets

Enjoy crafting clever gifts that are ever so thoughtful, and ever so easy.

QUICK TO STITCH

Ribbon with individual holiday motifs makes it super simple to whip up clever gift card sleeves. Choose 2-inch-wide ribbon and cut off a 3¼-inch segment, removing wire if edged in wire. Use embroidery floss to enhance the design with simple stitches as shown. Fold under the cut ends; press. Place the ribbon on felt and stitch around edges using zigzag stitches. Leaving a ½-inch border, trim around the edge with pinking shears. Leaving the top open, machine-stitch the layered piece to contrasting felt using a straight stitch. Trim around the edge leaving a ¼-inch border at the sides and bottom and an arch at the top.

LINE UP STRAIGHT

A dollar store tray gets a merry makeover lined with cheery holiday ribbons. Cut enough ribbon pieces to line the tray. Working one piece at a time, brush decoupage medium on the tray. Place a ribbon on the decoupage medium; smooth ribbon. Continue adding decoupage medium and ribbons in this manner until the tray is lined. For a finished edge, hot-glue red-and-white baker's string along the ribbon edges. Let dry.

SIMPLY BEAUTIFUL

Whatever their reading pleasure, gift recipients will love having a special bookmark on hand. Cut a 9-inch length from 2¼-inch-wide ribbon. Fold under each end ½ inch; secure with cross-stitches at corners. Cut a 13-inch length of ¾-inch-wide contrasting ribbon. Fold under the top end ½ inch; tuck wide ribbon into fold. Center narrow ribbon atop wide and machine-stitch along the edge. Turn under ½ inch of the ribbon tail; secure by stitching on a small jingle bell. Stitch more jingle bells to the ribbon tail as desired.

MERRY GOES ROUND

Dress a round cork coaster for the holidays by adding simple trims. Put a dot of hot glue in the center of the cork; adhere upholstery cord. Wind the cord around the center, tacking down with hot glue, until the surface of the coaster is covered. Cut off the excess cord. Glue heavy-duty red-and-white bakers' string between the rounds of cord. Glue coaster to red felt; trim around circle using pinking shears. Tie a double ribbon bow from narrow ribbons; glue to edge of coaster.

Special Delivery

Holiday gifts deserve clever carriers to show their thoughtfulness. These clever wraps are sure to evoke smiles from every age.

O CHRISTMAS TREE

Step aside premade bow, this mini bottlebrush tree wins the package topper contest, hands down. For the mini bucket, spray-paint a medicine dispenser cup silver; let dry. Hot-glue a decorated bottlebrush tree in the center of the cup. Add a ribbon bow. Use hot glue to hold the decoration to the wrapped gift.

SNOW GAL SALLY

Ready to spread holiday spirit, this happy snow gal adds joy to any gift package—even a jelly jar or peanut can! To make the body, hot-glue two white ping-pong balls together. For the base, use a 1¼-inch-diameter donut bead. Glue the snow gal body to the bead. Using a fine-line black marking pen, draw eyes, mouth, and eyebrows on one ping-pong ball. For the hat cuff, glue a piece of silver chenille stem around the head. Wind red chenille stem around the top of the head to complete the hat, gluing as needed. Wrap a red-and-white chenille stem around the neck twice for the scarf. Use an awl to poke an arm hole on each side. Cut two 1½-inch pieces of black leather lacing; hot-glue one in each hole. Craft a tiny carrot nose from oven-bake clay; bake as directed by manufacturer. Hot-glue nose to face. Add stickers for buttons and hat trim. Top the hat with a bead. To add a snowy touch, run a bead of hot glue along the top of the nose and the top of the buttons; sprinkle with white glitter. Add a paper base if desired. Hot-glue the snow gal to the wrapped gift.

SHAKE IT UP

Fillable round disc ornaments are the secret ingredient in this fun gift wrap. Pull apart the ornament and set half aside. Use pliers to bend the hanger back and forth until it snaps off. Trace around the ornament on light blue cardstock; cut out circle. Trace a little less than half the ornament on white glitter paper; cut out. Use glue stick to adhere the glitter paper to the blue paper, aligning edge. Use holiday stickers to create a small scene on paper circle. Pour a tablespoon of Epsom salt in the center of the circle. Run a line of hot glue around the edge of the ornament half; press onto paper circle, aligning edge. For the base, wrap a 1½×2¾-inch box with silver wrapping paper. Trim with stickers. Use double-sided tape to hold the base and globe to the package top.

TOP IT OFF

Cupcake toppers bring fun dimension to small gift packages. Cut a piece of decorative paper to cover the box top; adhere with glue stick. Use your imagination to add to the theme of the toppers. Here we used a small section of dollhouse fencing and sticker ornaments. Decide on the arrangement, then hot-glue the pieces to the package top. If a snowy look is desired, add small amounts of hot glue where desired and sprinkle with white glitter.

LAST-MINUTE WINNER

Fancy Christmas tree garland can top several holiday packages with ease. Use wire cutters or scissors to cut apart segments of the garland. Wrap the gift and top with a wide ribbon. Hot-glue the garland piece to the ribbon.

Naturally Festive

WEE WONDERS

Great little gifts for coworkers and neighbors, you can make these darling holiday accents in just minutes. Hot-glue faux greenery and jingle bells in the nest. Add a bird ornament perched on the nest edge. Brush the top of a grapevine nest, greenery, and jingle bells with white paint; let dry.

SNACK STACK

Two small grapevine wreaths elevate a candy dish for an extra-special presentation. Wire same-size wreaths together. Lightly brush the wreaths with white paint and let dry. Wire a large ribbon bow to one side. Place a candy dish in the center.

BRING THE OUTDOORS IN

Large pinecones offer a great start to ornament making. Drill a tiny hole in the pinecone top. Twist in a screw eye; secure with instant glue if needed. Brush the pinecone lightly with white paint; let dry. Hot-glue a double ribbon bow to the top and faux berries in the center. Thread string through the screw eye to hang.

NATURE RING

A mini grapevine wreath makes a natural napkin ring all by itself. To dress it up further, hot-glue tiny pinecones, berries, and leaves to one section of the wreath. Lightly brush on white paint to lend a snowy look; let dry. Tie a ribbon to the center of the design.

FARMHOUSE FANCY

This easy-to-make wreath can be made any size and its appeal stays the same. Wire artificial greenery and pinecones to one half of a grapevine wreath. Brush white paint onto the wreath and pinecones; let dry. Tear fabric strips and tie into a bow. Hot-glue bow and candy canes to the wreath for the grand finale.

kids

SO MANY CLEVER IDEAS
Get ready to craft some
super-fun holiday trims
and treasures.

Limb Trim

Share your creativity by making awesome decorations for the Christmas tree.

POLKA-DOT TREE

Full of pattern and texture, this supersoft ornament can be made in whatever color combination you love most. For the tree, use a 4-inch-tall foam tree, trimming a larger tree if necessary. Wrap the foam piece with fleece, trim to fit, overlapping the seam; secure with map pins. Trim the bottom of the fabric ¾ inch below the bottom of the tree. Make a slit in fabric, every ½ inch, to the tree's edge. Hot-glue the fringes to the bottom of the tree, overlapping as you work. Hot-glue a 2-inch-diameter cork or cardboard circle to the bottom of the tree. Glue on a cork for the trunk; cover with fleece and using hot glue to secure. Trim the fabric even with the bottom of the trunk. Push in yellow map pins to resemble lights. For ornaments, poke white quilter's pins through tiny pom-poms and press into the fabric-covered foam. Use a larger pom-pom for the topper. For hanger, fold over a 6-inch piece of wire; twist ends together. Poke the wire ends into the point of the foam piece, adding hot glue to secure.

BOBBER BOBS

Lightweight fishing bobbers make the perfect base for delightful snowmen ornaments. Press the button on a fishing bobber to push up the wire to secure the center of a 10-inch piece of heavy baker's string; knot the ends. Use a fine-tip black marking pen to draw a snowman face on the white section of the bobber. Hot-glue a tiny orange pom-pom nose. Hot-glue a pom-pom between the top strings. Trim the red hat brim with baker's string. Cut a 1×7-inch piece of fabric for scarf. Tie a loose knot in the center of the fabric. Insert the bobber button into the knot; hot-glue to secure.

CUSTOM BUILT

Paint cardboard tubes the desired colors; let dry. Cut an eraser into rectangles to use as stamps for windows. Dip the eraser piece into paint that contrasts the house and press onto the tube; let dry. Use cupcake liners to make roofs. For each roof, cut a liner from the outside edge to the center. Wrap the cut edges over each other and secure with an adhesive dot. Knot string ends, then thread the loop end through the top of the roof.

MR. FROSTY

A grapevine nest makes an unexpected head for a snowman.

WHAT YOU NEED
Grapevine bird nest
Paintbrush
Acrylic paint in white, orange, and black
Three large black map pins
Hot-glue gun and glue sticks
Toothpick
Fabric
Empty cardboard ribbon spool
Pencil
Straight edge
Scissors
Crafts knife
Cardstock
Hat trims
Decoupage medium
White glitter
10-inch piece of string

WHAT YOU DO
1. Brush the bottom of the nest with white paint; let dry.
2. Use large map pins for the eyes and nose; hot-glue in place. Paint the nose orange. Let the paint dry. To add highlights, dip the tip of a toothpick into white paint; add two dots to each eye and the nose as shown.
3. Cut a ½×6-inch piece of fabric; tie into a bow. Hot-glue bow at bottom of nest slightly off center.
4. For hat, use an empty ribbon spool as shown in Photo A. If you don't have one, you can improvise a cut-off mailing tube and lightweight cardboard circles.
5. Using a straight edge, draw a line across the center of one end of the spool as shown in Photo B.
6. On the other end of the spool, cut off the excess cardboard flush to the tube as shown in Photo C.
7. Using a crafts knife and following the drawn line to start, cut the spool in half as shown in Photo D.
8. Aligning the straight edge of the tube's small end and the edge of the cardstock, trace around the half circle as shown in Photo E.

9. Cut out the shape from cardstock. Hot-glue the shape on top of the hat as shown in Photo F.
10. Paint the hat black; let dry.
11. Cut a fabric band, approximately ¾-inches wide and long enough to wrap hat, and hot-glue it to the hat above the brim.
12. Glue mini holiday trims to the right side of the hat.

13. Brush decoupage medium on the top hat seam and the trims; sprinkle with glitter.
14. Thread string through the top of the nest; knot ends to secure.
15. Hot-glue the hat to the snowman. If the trim tips forward, hot-glue the string hanger to the hat as needed.

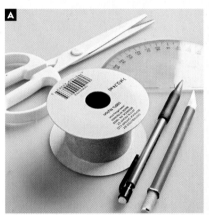

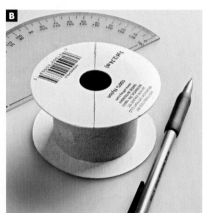

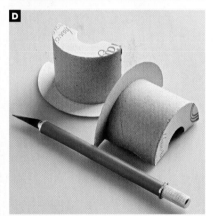

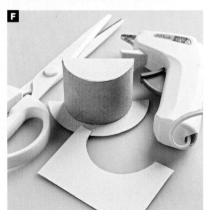

Kids on a Roll

Save cardboard rolls from the recycling bin and use them to print one-of-a-kind seasonal place mats and wrapping supplies.

HOLLY JOLLY WREATH

Bragging rights will be all yours when guests admire your handiwork bringing cheer to the front door.

WHAT YOU NEED
Cutting board
Table knife
Tape measure
3-inch-long piece of 1-inch-diameter wood dowel
Foam pool noodles in green, red, and white
Scissors
Hot-glue gun and glue sticks
Decorative tulle ribbon in red and pink
Fishing line

WHAT YOU DO
1. Cover the work surface with a cutting board. Measure and cut a 56-inch-long piece from green noodle with a table knife. To help the tube form a wreath shape, use the knife to cut slits halfway through the tube, approximately every inch. Put hot glue on one end of dowel, push half of the dowel into one end of the tube. With the slits on the outside, repeat for the other side to form a ring.
2. For holly shapes, cut 4-inch-long pieces of green noodle; cut in half lengthwise. Use scissors to clip off the corners, making pointed ends. (NOTE: The wreath shown uses approximately 27 wreath shapes.) Hot-glue the holly to the wreath front, placing some in groupings and pointing in various directions.
3. To make the flowers, cut ½-inch-thick slices from a red noodle. Glue groups of threes and single blooms onto the holly. To make the centers, cut ¼-inch-thick slices from red; cut in half. Coil the pieces and glue them inside the flowers.
4. For white loops, cut ¼-inch-thick slices from white; cut in half. Glue the ends together. Glue the white loops by the flowers. Fill in the wreath with random snippets of green noodle.
5. Cut two 36-inch lengths from each color of tulle. Stack pieces together and use to tie a bow around the wreath. Fluff out the loops.
6. Tie fishing line at the top to hang.

TOO CUTE TO EAT

This familiar symbol of the holiday season gets super-sized attention. Crafted from new foam pool noodles, the trim is light enough to hang just about anywhere.

WHAT YOU NEED
Cutting board
Table knife
Tape measure
Foam pool noodles in red, green, and white
Heavy-duty wire
Wire cutters
Hot-glue gun and glue sticks
1-inch-wide white grosgrain ribbon
Jumbo white rickrack
Scissors
Chenille stems in white and red
½-inch dowel
Fishing line

WHAT YOU DO
1. Cover the work surface with a cutting board. To make a candy cane, use a table knife to cut a 45-inch length from a red foam pool noodle. Ask an adult to cut a 20-inch length of heavy-duty wire. Insert the wire into the foam tube, so that the wire end is approximately an inch inside the tube end. Carefully bend the tube and wire to make a candy cane shape.
2. To make stripes, hot-glue 1-inch-wide white grosgrain ribbon to one end of the candy cane. Wrap the tube at a diagonal, spacing stripes approximately 2½ inches apart. Fill in between the stripes with white jumbo rickrack.
3. To make the center embellishment, slice off 4- to 8-inch-long pieces from green and white noodles. Cut in half lengthwise. Cut each piece in half again. Use scissors to make short snips along the long edges, being careful not to cut too close to the center. Trim the ends into points. For round flowers, slice ½-inch pieces from white and green noodles. For flower centers, cut narrow slices from contrasting noodles, cut in half, roll up, and insert into the hole in the flower. To make a petalled flower, cut ½-inch slices from a white noodle in halves. Bend each piece in half; poke a white chenille stem through the sides near the fold. When all five pieces are threaded

onto the chenille stem, snug the pieces together and twist the chenille stem ends to secure; cut off excess. Hot-glue a green coil in the center.
4. To attach the trims, start with the long pieces of green and white tube. Arrange and hot-glue the pieces to the candy cane. Add the flowers. For the coils, wrap red chenille stems around a ½-inch dowel; remove. Glue the ends of the stems to the center arrangement.
5. Tie fishing line to the top to hang the adornment.

SMILIN' SNOW FOLKS

A single white foam pool noodle, cut into slices, can be the start of dozens of personality-filled ornaments. To make a snow person, slice off a ½-inch-thick segment from a pool noodle using a table knife. Cut an orange chenille stem in half; coil one segment. Using a pencil, push out center to make a carrot nose shape. Hot-glue the nose in the center of the foam slice. For eyes, cut two 1-inch-long pieces of black chenille stem; shape into crescents. Fold under ⅓ of stem on both ends. Gently press the eyes into place. For mouth, cut five ½-inch pieces of black chenille stem; fold each in half. Push the first mouth piece into the foam below the nose. Add two on each side, arranging in a smile formation. Use your imagination to form a hat and scarf from pre-twisted chenille stems, using the photo as inspiration. Hot-glue the accessories in place. To add a hanger, hot-glue a string loop to the back.

RISE TO THE OCCASION

So cute adorning the table, these place card holders could just as easily lift up a heartfelt sentiment to enjoy every day of the holiday season. To make a holder, protect the work surface with a cutting board. Use a table knife to cut a ½-inch slice from a white foam pool noodle, a ¾-inch slice from a red noodle, and a very narrow slice from green. Make a ½-inch-deep cut into one side of the red noodle piece. Use scissors to cut little whisps from the green slice to resemble evergreen. With the cut side up, hot-glue the red noodle to the center of the white noodle. Cut three 1-inch pieces of red chenille stem and three 2-inch pieces from red-and-white chenille stem. Wrap each red piece around a skewer to make a small round berry shape; remove. Shape each red-and-white piece into a loop. Referring to the photo for placement, glue the chenille stem pieces to the white base. Fill in with green whisps. Cut a 1×3-inch place card from white card stock for each base. Write the guest's name on the card and slip it into the slot.

NORTH POLE SNOWFLAKES

Just like the real things, these snowflakes show off different patterns—each one beautiful in its own way. Use white foam pool noodles and white chenille stems to make these pretty designs inspired by Mother Nature. Look at the photo for inspiration. We used whole, half, and quarter circles, plus thinly sliced half circles gathered at the ends to create petal shapes. Cut several ½- and ¼-inch-thick slices. Lay out a pattern and cut chenille stems to connect the pieces. For a snowy look, lay the snowflakes on a protected work surface and gently spray with a thin layer of artificial snow.

ALL LIT UP

Make the season bright with a wall tree trimmed with Christmas tree bulbs. To make the tree, cut a green foam pool noodle into these lengths: 14, 12, 10, 8, 6, 4, and 2 inches. Arrange the pieces in tree formation; run a line of hot glue in each seam to secure pieces together (this will be the back side). To back each lightbulb, cut a thin slice from a white pool noodle; trim around the edge using pinking shears. Use a table knife to cut an X where each bulb is desired. Slip a white backer onto the threaded end of the bulb and gently push the bulb into the X. Continue adding bulbs until all Xs are filled. To add interest, cut thin slices from green noodle. Trim the edge using pinking shears and cut from the outside edge to the inside circle. Coil the foam piece; secure end with hot glue. Place the coils in the creases of the tree using hot glue to secure. For the trunk, cut a 6-inch piece from a red noodle. Cut a curve in one end to fit the bottom of the tree; hot-glue in place.

Note: Please use caution when handling lightbulbs. Use new, heavy-duty bulbs. Do not use thin or brittle bulbs.

Put a Spell on It

Personalize handmade gifts using alphabet letters to spell the names of family and friends or to add a seasonal sentiment.

RESERVED FOR SANTA

Greet jolly ol' St. Nick with a cookie plate made just for him. Using alphabet beads, string SANTA onto a 6-inch piece of wire, stringing contrasting beads between the letters. Add larger beads on each end. Bend the wire to follow the curve of a paper plate rim. Use a small paper punch to make a pair of holes where the beads end. Thread the wire ends through the holes and bend the wires under the plate to secure.

SWEET AND HEARTFELT

Surprise family and friends with personalized candy cane hearts. Arrange two candy canes to form a heart; join with hot glue. Using alphabet beads, thread a friend's or family member's name onto a silver chenille stem. Slide beads to the center. Add decorative beads on each side of alphabet beads if desired. Arrange the chenille stem diagonally on the heart and gently wrap the ends around the candy cane.

VERY MERRY NECKLACE

Cut a 36-inch length of beading thread; insert one end through a beading needle. Thread on a jingle bell and slide it to the center of thread. Insert the loose thread end into the needle to secure the jingle bell in the loop. Lay out the desired bead design, including alphabet beads spelling Merry in the center. String on the beads, from the bottom of design, onto the thread. Once the bottom section is complete, remove one of the threads from the needle. Thread on upper necklace beads to the back center; remove needle. Thread opposite thread into the needle and repeat the bead design; remove needle. Knot the thread ends together securely; cut off thread tails.

NAME THAT GIFT

In minutes you can make gift "tags" that are sure to be kept even after the gift opening is over. Simply thread alphabet beads onto short pieces of ball chain and hook clasp. Loop the ring around the gift package bow.

INVITING EVERGREENS

Set the holiday table with graphic tree place cards labeled with alphabet bead trunks. Use marking pens to draw horizontal lines in shades of green. Use the patterns on page 158 to cut one large and two small trees for each card. For card base, cut a 3½×4-inch piece from white card stock; fold with short ends together. Using the photo as a guide, glue the trees to the place card using a glue stick. Thread alphabet beads onto wire, spelling each guest's name. Use an awl to poke two holes in the large tree, the first just below the bottom edge of the tree. Thread the bottom wire through the hole; fold upward to secure. Poke the second hole just above the top bead. Thread the wire through the hole; bend downward to secure.

Sweet Sensations

HOLLY AND BERRIED CANES

Tiny accents dress up candy canes in a hurry. Hot-glue an artificial holly sprig to a wrapped candy cane, a little higher than half the way up the straight part of the candy cane. Tie a ribbon bow around the candy cane to cover the holly stem.

LOLLIPOP DROP

As pretty as ice crystals, rock candy on sticks transform easily into ornaments for the tree. For each trim, cut an 8-inch length of baker's string; knot ends together. Lay the candy stick on top of the string, slip the knotted end through the loop, and pull the cut ends to secure the hanger just below the wood ball at the stick's end. Tie a ribbon bow at the top of the handle. Hot-glue a small jingle bell in the center of the bow.

BITS AND PIECES

Candy garlands can last years or get eaten as soon as the Christmas tree comes down. This garland showcases peppermint balls and candy stick pieces. But visit any candy store to discover limitless options. Simply tie pieces together, leaving space between, using heavy baker's string.

PEPPERMINTS ALL AROUND

Combine candies to make jolly mini wreath ornaments. Unwrap seven green peppermint discs; arrange in a circle on a protected work surface. Run a line of hot glue around the candy circle. Place a 2-inch metal ring into the glue to hold the candies in place; let cool. Turn the candy wreath over. Hot-glue a cinnamon imperial in the center of each peppermint. Tie a ribbon bow and hot-glue to the wreath. Tie baker's string to the top to hang.

patterns

EMBROIDERY STITCH DIAGRAMS

FRENCH KNOT DIAGRAM

RUNNING STITCH DIAGRAM

STRAIGHT STITCH DIAGRAM

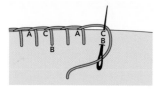

BLANKET STITCH DIAGRAM

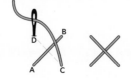

CROSS-STITCH DIAGRAM

LAZY DAISY STITCH DIAGRAM

HOW TO MAKE A TASSEL

1. Wrap yarn many times around cardboard. Tie into a bundle at one end; cut other end (A).
2. Wrap yarn around the bundle several times near the tied end; tie in place (B).
3. Trim the loose ends of the yarn to the desired tassel length (C).

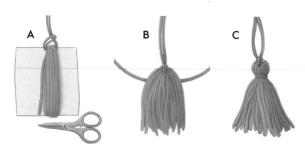

HOW TO MAKE A POM-POM

1. Wrap yarn many times around a piece of cardboard, fork, book, or other object depending on the size of pom-pom desired (A).
2. Tie the entire bundle in the center and slide the yarn from the object (B).
3. Cut the looped yarn at both ends of the bundle (C).
4. Trim yarn ends to desired length (D) and fluff the yarn.

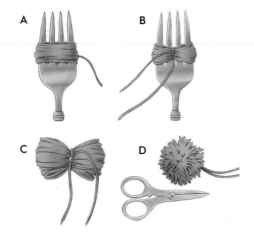

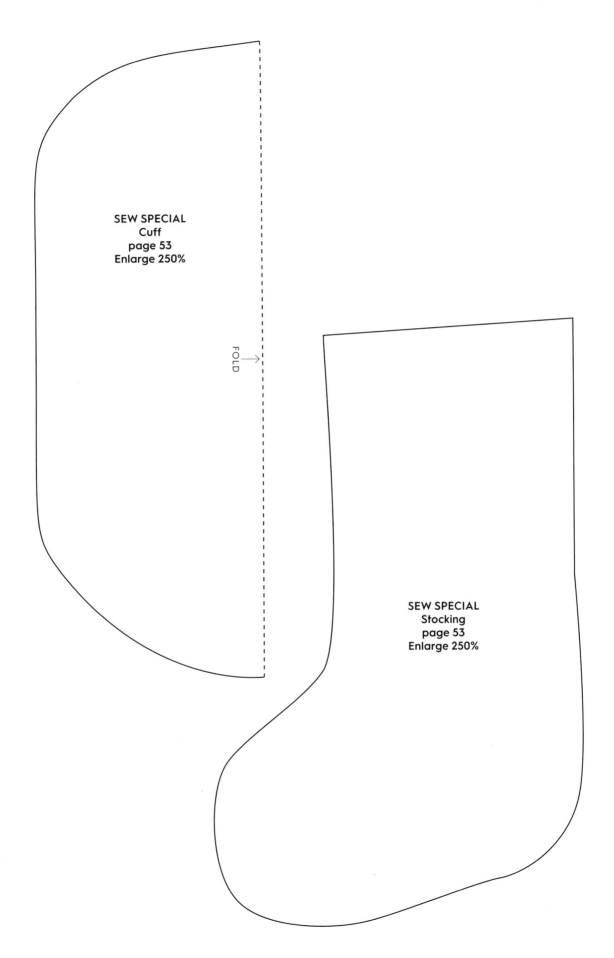

SEW SPECIAL
Cuff
page 53
Enlarge 250%

FOLD →

SEW SPECIAL
Stocking
page 53
Enlarge 250%

Patterns

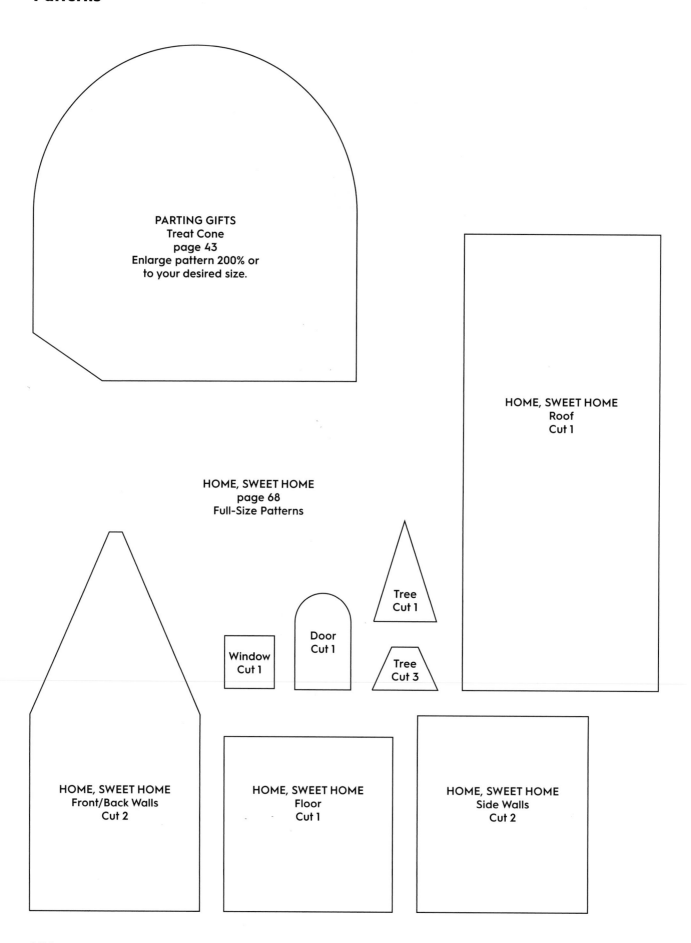

PARTING GIFTS
Treat Cone
page 43
Enlarge pattern 200% or
to your desired size.

HOME, SWEET HOME
Roof
Cut 1

HOME, SWEET HOME
page 68
Full-Size Patterns

Tree
Cut 1

Window
Cut 1

Door
Cut 1

Tree
Cut 3

HOME, SWEET HOME
Front/Back Walls
Cut 2

HOME, SWEET HOME
Floor
Cut 1

HOME, SWEET HOME
Side Walls
Cut 2

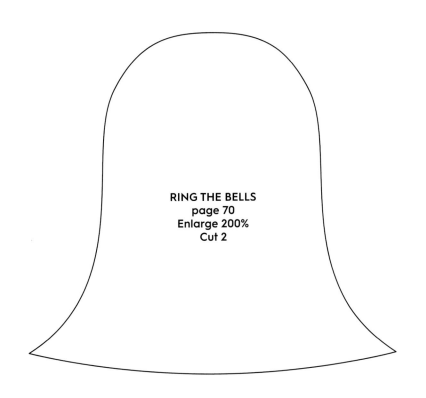

RING THE BELLS
page 70
Enlarge 200%
Cut 2

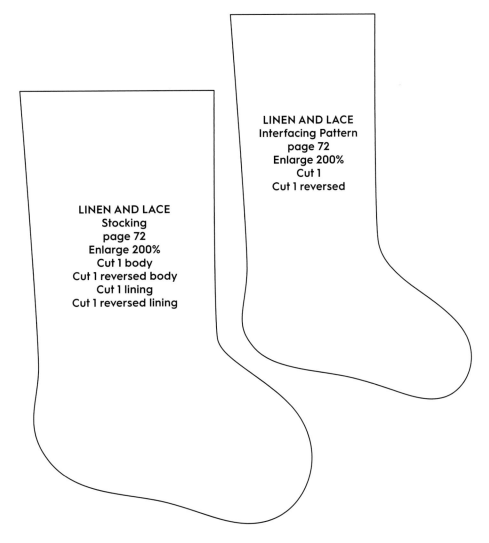

LINEN AND LACE
Stocking
page 72
Enlarge 200%
Cut 1 body
Cut 1 reversed body
Cut 1 lining
Cut 1 reversed lining

LINEN AND LACE
Interfacing Pattern
page 72
Enlarge 200%
Cut 1
Cut 1 reversed

Patterns

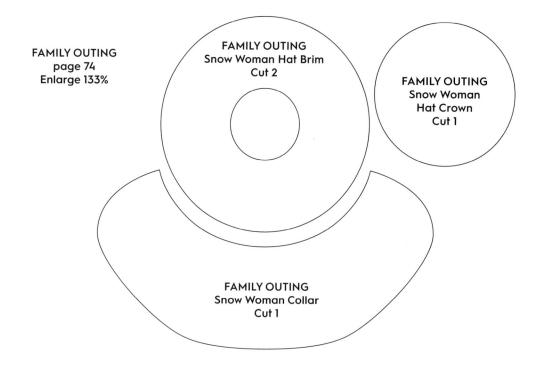

FAMILY OUTING
page 74
Enlarge 133%

FAMILY OUTING
Snow Woman Hat Brim
Cut 2

FAMILY OUTING
Snow Woman
Hat Crown
Cut 1

FAMILY OUTING
Snow Woman Collar
Cut 1

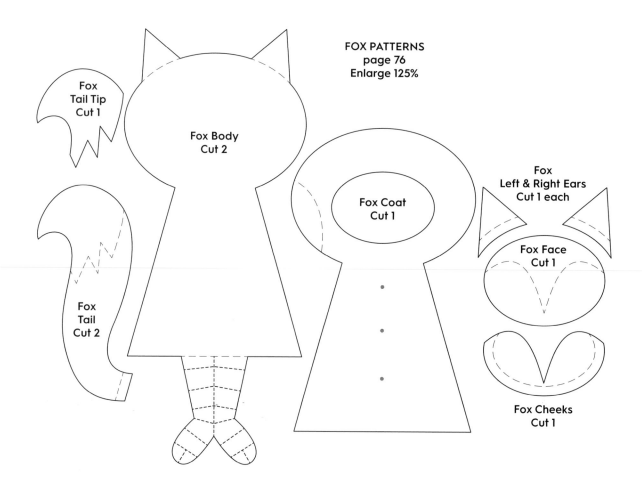

FOX PATTERNS
page 76
Enlarge 125%

Fox
Tail Tip
Cut 1

Fox Body
Cut 2

Fox Coat
Cut 1

Fox
Left & Right Ears
Cut 1 each

Fox
Tail
Cut 2

Fox Face
Cut 1

Fox Cheeks
Cut 1

LLAMA LOVE
page 77
Full-Size Patterns

Heart
Cut 1

Saddle
Cut 1

Llama Body
Cut 2

COME ON OVER
Invitation graphic
page 78
Enlarge to your
desired size.

Patterns

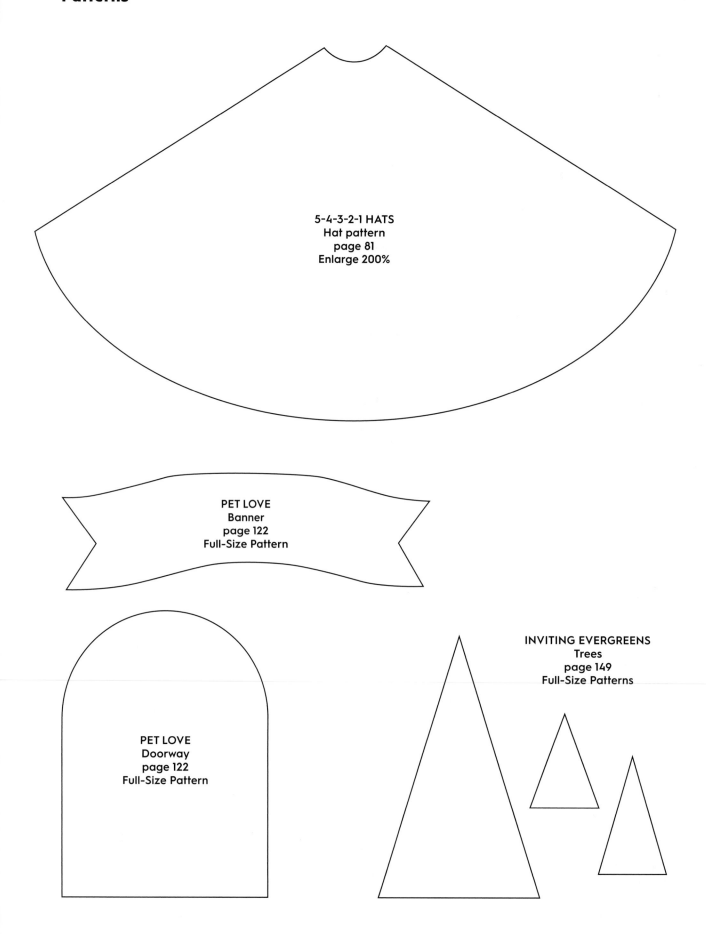

5-4-3-2-1 HATS
Hat pattern
page 81
Enlarge 200%

PET LOVE
Banner
page 122
Full-Size Pattern

PET LOVE
Doorway
page 122
Full-Size Pattern

INVITING EVERGREENS
Trees
page 149
Full-Size Patterns

index

Index

RECIPES

CREDITS

Photo Styling
Sue Banker

Photography
Marty Baldwin
Jason Donnelly
Jacob Fox
Brie Passano
Ken Carlson